Innovation Soup

Innovation Soup

A Recipe for Organizational Success

Sanjay Puligadda, PhD and Don Waisanen, PhD

BUSINESS EXPERT PRESS

Leader in applied, concise business books

Innovation Soup: A Recipe for Organizational Success

Cover design by Sanjida Smrity

Interior design by Exeter Premedia Services Private Ltd., Chennai, India

First published in 2022 by
Business Expert Press, LLC
222 East 46th Street, New York, NY 10017
www.businessexpertpress.com

ISBN-13: 978-1-63742-305-9 (paperback)
ISBN-13: 978-1-63742-306-6 (e-book)

Business Expert Press Human Resource Management and Organizational
Behavior Collection

First edition: 2022

10 9 8 7 6 5 4 3 2 1

Description

Not your average cookbook. This is a research-based recipe for innovation!

This book is for anyone wanting to kick-start innovation in their organization. It is ground-breaking in two ways:

- It is based on data, combining empirical research, literature reviews, business cases, and interviews.
- It tells a story of two friends in diametrically opposite business predicaments due to Covid. Their story is complex and layered, making for an engaging reading.

For too long, innovation culture has been amorphous. InnoQ™, built on years of rigorous research, breaks innovation into 11 dimensions that can be measured, tracked, and improved. We share real world data and examples showing the power of the 11 dimensions and provide concrete ways to improve on them. The pandemic has fundamentally changed the way organizations do business for the next many years—creating a culture of innovation is now more important than ever.

This book is perfect for leaders, innovators, managers, and students.

Keywords

innovation; organizational culture; measurement; collaboration; empathy; diversity; creativity; high-performing organization; improvisation; leadership

Contents

Preface

This book delivers a rigorous, data-based approach to building a culture of innovation in your organization. To make the extensive research and the data behind this book palatable and digestible, we have intentionally packaged the information in an engaging story format. The book begins with the story of Peter and David, two friends who find themselves in diametrically opposite business predicaments due to the Covid pandemic, because of differences in innovation culture. Their story is layered and complex—it's a tale of frustration, friendship, rivalry, and respect. An innovation consultant, Laura, could be a beacon of hope. But is she able to help? We invite you to read on to find out.

We use the story of Peter, David and Laura, as it unfolds, to layer in an exegesis of the 11 dimensions of innovation culture. We explain the extensive research that went into a diagnostic tool for measuring innovation culture called the InnoQ™ and describe how it can be used to improve innovation culture. We share real world data showing the power of the 11 dimensions and how they can be used to benchmark innovation culture. We also suggest concrete ways to make changes and improve on the dimensions to get your "innovation soup" right.

For too long, innovation culture has been amorphous and hard-to-define. Grounded in research, this book offers a straightforward and practical framework for assessing, tracking, and improving innovation culture. We have packaged its contents in an easy-to-read format, focusing on how to implement this work—starting tomorrow—above all else.

As a McKinsey report recently stated, "prioritizing innovation is the key to unlocking postcrisis growth," with a survey finding that most (90 percent) managers are convinced that the pandemic will fundamentally change the way they do business for the next many years.[1] Understanding

---

[1] "Innovation in a Crisis: Why it is More Critical than Ever," *McKinsey & Company*, June 17, 2020. www.mckinsey.com/business-functions/strategy-and-corporate-finance/our-insights/innovation-in-a-crisis-why-it-is-more-critical-than-ever.

and building an organization's innovation capabilities is now more important than ever.

There are many books on innovation. There are three ways this book is different:

- It is based on a thorough data-collection and analysis conducted by the first author, case examples from companies, and the research and experiences of both authors.
- Every chapter starts in a novel, narrative format designed to get readers' attention using a continuing story that makes the information relatable and memorable.
- We know how busy you are! We are too. As such, we have attempted to keep everything brief, compelling, and practical. While packing in information along the way, our chapters are short, and get to the point with key takeaways and action items provided.

PART 1

Setting Up

CHAPTER 1

A Tale of Two Companies

"15 years, David!"

"I know! They were fantastic years Phil! I can't thank you enough for all those years of hard work," said David, looking into Phil's eyes.

"You know our situation," he continued with a tone of desperation and despair. "I really don't have any other choice. I am sorry." He meant it. He really liked Phil. He hated letting anyone go, much less Phil. Over the years, their families had gotten to know each other. He and Phil also shared a passion for beer. They would often head out after work to try out a new brewery and had become great friends over many a pint.

They were seated in David's office, a well-appointed room on the c-suite corner of the fourth floor of an austere building that served as corporate headquarters for his company. A balding man in his 50s, David was dressed in a tie, khaki pants, and a pressed shirt. He had kind eyes, a bulging mid-section, and a warm, effusive manner. He was liked by his employees, although he often wondered if they respected him.

There was a lot Phil wanted to say. He was experiencing a range of emotions: anger, frustration, disappointment, and hurt. He was hurting more than anything else. He had given the best years of his life to this company and now he was just being let go by someone he thought was his friend. He was seething but looking across the table he could feel David's discomfort. Deep down he knew David hated doing this but had no choice—given the circumstances, this wasn't a surprise. He just couldn't bring himself up to saying anything. He just got up and left the room, slamming the door on his way out.

This was the third team member David was letting go this week. Covid-19 had devastated his small manufacturing business that made kitchen supplies. His customers' customers kept away almost completely, which meant his customers were keeping away from him. It was fast. His orders just melted away and he just couldn't afford his team anymore.

Like most small businesses (< 500 employees), he had less than 15 days of cash reserves. Credit also became tighter. The situation had lasted much longer than David had anticipated. Although he was getting some government loans from the pandemic, he still had to cut his labor.

He had inherited this business from his father, Steve, a second-generation Greek immigrant who had worked hard to establish this company. A hard working, ambitious man, Steve had an iron grip at work and home. David grew up in his shadow. Steve was regimented and set in his ways, single handedly building his business from scratch. Up until his death a year ago, his footprint could be seen in every aspect of the business.

In another part of the town, there was a similar office in a similar building. Peter was seated in his room on the c-suite corner of his offices. Peter was also in his early 50s, an energetic, charismatic CEO of his uniform-production company. He was also well liked by his team.

"Nice work! Things have been great this past quarter!" said Peter to a loud cheer from his team gathered in the conference room.

"We have reached another milestone. I can't believe Covid-19 did not affect us at all. We were able to pivot and come around shining."

He was addressing his second quarter meeting of 2021. His uniform-production company had made exciting changes in the past few months. Up until Covid, its biggest customers were bars and restaurants. The company had gone through some amazing transformations in business process to adjust to life with the coronavirus and to changing customer demands. It had been nimble and fast, and found an innovative way to keep afloat.

The meeting was going well. There was a sense of celebration, of relief at having survived a pandemic and coming out on top, and a general feeling of hope for the future in a post-Covid world. Even though a variant of the virus was threatening the public again, the staff's innovations had made sure the company would continue to perform well. The mood was celebratory and effusive. There was cake, hors d'oeuvres, and champagne. The festivities of Peter's meeting made it stretch far longer than the one David had in his office.

David was scheduled to meet Peter that evening for happy hour in the brewery down the street, but Peter texted that he was running late from wrapping up his team's meeting. Peter and David knew each other from their MBA days. They had both enrolled in evening MBA classes at the Ohio State University. They often carpooled from Cincinnati, where they lived, to Columbus. They had also been class and project mates. Being business owners (a relative minority in their class of working professionals), they had decided to stay in touch. Although in aligned industries, they were not competitors. David had inherited his business from his family, while Peter started it on his own.

Having concluded his day early, David drove over to the brewery, deciding to wait for Peter if he was going to be late. The meeting with Phil had rattled him and he needed a drink. Sol was one of the many new breweries that had mushroomed recently. Set back from the street, the brewery was housed in a former factory with tall ceilings, large windows, and a warm, welcoming vibe. The bar was on one end of the cavernous hall. Although it was early, the crowd was already starting to pick up. He walked up and ordered a small flight of beers. He liked tasting the new beers on tap before picking one. Picking up his flight he sat down to wait for his buddy.

After what seemed like an interminable wait, Peter walked in. David stood and waved. Spotting him, Peter started toward his table. He looked happy and excited.

"You look ecstatic," said David. The warm handshake that they usually greeted each other with was now gone, ravaged by two years of a relentless pandemic. Just like everyone around them, the two buddies were now used to not shaking hands.

Peter gave him an affectionate look before saying, "We just celebrated a fantastic quarter!"

"Good for you," said David, grudgingly.

"How're things with you?" asked Peter.

"Why don't you get your beer, and we can chat?"

"Sure. Be right back," said Peter. He bounded off to the bar, placed his order, and came back to the table with his IPA.

"I just fired my third guy this week."

"Oops," said Peter, not knowing quite what to say. There was a brief silence. Peter had known things were not going very well for David.

"Sorry to hear that man. Cheers?" he said, nervously trying to lighten the mood.

David did not reply. Instead, he took a long sip of his beer. After a moment's pause, he finally said, "Cheers to you! You guys just celebrated a great quarter!"

"We did."

"How did you guys do it?" asked David.

Peter shrugged his shoulders, trying to be modest.

"What's going on man?" continued David. "I am screwed, you are partying!"

"I don't know dude. Luck? Different industry?"

David shook his head. "Don't be modest or gracious. I think I know what it is…"

"And that is . . .?"

"Culture. There is something about your company. I have always felt it. There is an energy, a spirit. It always felt like your people could take risks, that they enjoyed challenges, and there was a spirit of collaboration."

"You are too kind," said Peter, a little embarrassed. He felt bad for his friend and wondered if the success of his own company was making matters worse.

"I inherited my company from my old man," said David. "He had very clear views on how to run things. Until pretty much last year, he was into everything there. I don't blame him; it was his baby. But I feel like there is an outdated, stifling culture—a lack of openness and change. He was just not into that stuff."

"Lots of companies have suffered at the hands of Covid," said Peter.

"I know but we could have done better."

"I think you are being too hard on yourself David."

"I don't think so Peter," said David, taking the last sip of his taster. "I need more beer. Would you like another?"

"I am okay thanks."

"Be right back."

Peter hoped David wasn't about to get drunk. He felt that for David, the firing of his third employee this week was bad enough, but what was making it worse was how well business was going for his friend. Peter blamed himself for sounding celebratory this evening. He remembered back to the David he knew from his class days. He was competitive and especially liked to do better than Peter on every assignment.

David came back with his beer. Without waiting a second, he continued. "I also tried my best. I spent money on R&D, hired an innovation manager. Set up incentives for innovation, nothing really worked. I do think there is something in a company's culture dude. Something impermeable, something palpable. A sort of personality, a soul."

Peter nodded pensively.

David, in his usual acerbic manner, said "It's like two people having the exact same circumstances but, due to some special sauce, one comes out ahead whereas the other is devastated."

*   *   *

Okay, let's stop here. While this story is fictitious, there is more to what the two gentlemen above are talking about than many may realize. Let's see if David might have a point.

David's organization had not made any efforts to diversify its offerings, grow and expand, or find new customers or markets. The company was very set in its ways, confident in its way of doing things but not ready to try out new ideas and actions. It worked fine until the environment threw a challenge at it—Covid.

Peter's company was facing the same headwinds as David's, and yet it had flourished. Is it possible then that the culture of Peter and his team really made the difference? Given the largely simultaneous effects of Covid on both their companies, is it at all possible that there was a difference in their cultures that led to different outcomes? At a minimum, it seems one was able to innovate while the other couldn't.

CHAPTER 2

The Soup

How is creating an innovative organization like making soup?

Innovation is often put on a pedestal. There is a voluminous literature on innovation—both academic and practitioner. In fact, there are scores of business books with innovation in the title. The interest in innovation is not surprising, as everyone wants to innovate. And a good case can be made that a failure to innovate will sound the death knell for any organization. Just ask David.

However, innovation is not like a predictable assembly line or a precisely controlled procedure that can be switched on at will. According to Matt Ridley in *How Innovation Works: And Why It Flourishes in Freedom,* which chronicles the history of the concept, innovation is an incremental, bottom-up, almost serendipitous process rather than a procedure developed according to a fixed plan.[1] He says that it is always a collective, collaborative phenomenon, not a matter of lonely genius. The author bases his lessons on tracking the genesis, evolution, and ultimate outcomes of scores of actual innovations. Creating the right conditions for innovation can only happen when a mix of collective forces are at play.

True innovation does not come from a single individual, even if that individual is Peter from the story mentioned earlier, or Steve Jobs. It does not come from a single event or initiative or investment. Innovation is not precise, nor perfectly programmable. There is empirical support for this suggestion, with studies showing that the innovation process as it unfolds over time is messy, iterative, and often involves two steps forward, one step backward, and several steps to the side.[2]

---

[1] M. Ridley. 2020. *How Innovation Works: And Why it Flourishes in Freedom* (New York, NY: Harper).

[2] A. Van de Ven, H. Angle, and M.S. Poole. 1989. *Research on the Management of Innovation* (New York, NY: Harper and Row).

True, repeatable innovation is collaborative, and bottom up; it is holistic, organic, and ongoing. Creating an innovative organization, in that sense, is like making soup—*a soup of ingredients that, if given just the right stir and sustained over time, will create the kind of collaborative, high-performing organization that every person should aspire to being a part of and building.* There is a need for the right environment, ingredients, and processes, with a need to taste and adjust and keep the pot boiling. It's all in the culture of the organization. The culture is the soup.

Based on extensive research, the first author (Sanjay) found 11 dimensions of innovation culture that are the key ingredients for innovation soup. Without these, no fancy equipment or tools or investments are going to do it. Whether you're starting a new company or seeking to reboot your organization's culture to be innovation ready, this book will show you the ingredients and recipe for creating this soup.

Another way of looking at this is that if you *don't* have a plan for building and sustaining an innovative culture, there is simply no way to be effective in the longer term. In the words of Tony Hsieh, the late CEO of Zappos,

> Our number one priority is company culture. Our whole belief is that if you get the culture right, most of the other stuff like delivering great customer service or building a long-term enduring brand will just happen naturally on its own.[3]

Zappos invests heavily in employee team building and culture promotion. The company is also so sure that employees will like and advance its culture that it offers $4,000 to new hires to quit!

Hsieh is not alone. Didier Elzinga, CEO of Culture Amp said, "We believe to be successful; you need to put culture first."[4] Brian Chesky, the

[3] "Zappos CEO Tony Hsieh: Full Interview Transcript," *Marketplace.* August 19, 2010. www.marketplace.org/2010/08/19/zappos-ceo-tony-hsieh-full-interview-transcript/.

[4] D. Elzinga. n.d. "What is a Culture First Company—And Why Does it Matter?," *Culture Amp.* www.cultureamp.com/blog/what-is-a-culture-first-company-and-why-does-it-matter.

CEO of Airbnb, wrote a provocatively titled article on *Medium* titled, "Don't F*%$ Up the Culture."[5] As he notes,

> The stronger the culture, the less corporate process a company needs. When the culture is strong, you can trust everyone to do the right thing. People can be independent and autonomous. They can be entrepreneurial. And if we have a company that is entrepreneurial in spirit, we will be able to take our next "(wo) man on the moon" leap.

Innovation culture starts from the top. Top leadership needs to create a culture where success and failures are rewarded. We interviewed Dr. Shekhar Mitra,[6] former senior vice president of Global Innovation at Procter & Gamble (P&G) about his experiences on this aspect of the culture and its importance in driving significant innovation. Shekhar was associated with and led several breakthrough innovations in the industry including Aleve, Prilosec, and Crest Whitestrips.

He recalled his experiences on the cultural elements of the organization—the ability to learn fast from failures, the drive for reiterative design and prototyping, and complete transparency and open communication with teams and leaders on data and learning. During the early development of both Aleve and Prilosec, the FDA advisory committee was not satisfied with the sufficiency of efficacy and safety data submitted, sending teams back to the drawing board to design additional clinical and consumer label comprehension studies to ensure appropriate OTC (over the counter) medication standards were followed. Similarly, the tooth whitening Crest Whitestrips went through many iterations in design to ensure superior ease of use and noticeable efficacy. In all these instances, what

---

[5] B. Chesky. April 20, 2014. "Don't Fuck Up the Culture," *Medium*. https://medium.com/@bchesky/dont-fuck-up-the-culture-597cde9ee9d4.

[6] In an interview with S. Mitra, former senior vice president of Global Innovation and a member of P&G's top leadership team, the Global Leadership Council. Post retirement from P&G, he has spent seven years as a board member and strategic advisor to several F500 companies and new ventures. www.linkedin.com/in/shekhar-mitra-ph-d-4b427b47/.

initially appeared to be setbacks and failures led to a much better offering to the consumer.

As Shekhar recalled, in all the examples, leadership was fully committed to the process. The pushback (e.g., from the FDA) and the iterations needed were not seen as failures but a path to provide the best offering consistent with the values and mission of the company. Team members were supported and rewarded for this behavior to share learnings from both successes and failures and create the best design to delight the consumer.

Every leader needs to know the recipe for making sure their organizational culture is at its peak when it comes to innovation. Every employee of a business also needs to know what ingredients they should demand so that their workplaces are thriving rather than merely surviving.

Innovation Is Natural

As markets mature, as competition stiffens, as human desires and wants shift, there is no choice but to innovate. But still, does every factory, office, or organization need to be trained on innovation? If it is humans who are running all these factories and offices, and it is humanity's innovative capabilities that have brought us to where we are, why suddenly do we need all this literature and all these methods to train us on how to innovate?

Innovation is natural to us, just as creativity is. After all, creativity is the fuel that innovation runs on. Remember when we were children? We had active imaginations, thoughts, and said and did the craziest things. We built castles where there were none and turned trees into forts. We were geniuses at creativity, and then we went ahead and got educated. Don't just take our word for it; there's a boatload of research on this.[7]

It's the same thing with organizations. Entrepreneurs give birth to ideas that are, like children, a hotbed of creativity and then, while scaling up, they become too complex, bureaucratized, and complicated. At that point, they then feel the need to be "taught" how to innovate. They feel the need for interventions and specific initiatives.

---

[7] K. Robinson. 2011. *Out of our Minds: Learning to be Creative* (Hoboken, NJ: Capstone).

As the World Economic Forum report on "The Future of Jobs"[8] details, in a future replete with new products, technologies, and ways of working, creativity and innovation will increasingly be the most important need for organizations. However, being an innovative organization is not about having an innovation manager, nor is it about one's number of patents. True innovation is not orderly, nor can it be driven only by a specific division or champion. Innovation must be organization wide and reside in the DNA of an organization's culture. Research shows that a company's culture is, in fact, the biggest barrier to innovation, even with the right systems and resources in place.[9]

At the end of the day, organizations do not need to *do* so much as they need to *undo*. When training working executives to be creative, we ask them to "be like children" and undo some of the effects of their education and socialization processes. Similarly, organizations need to remove barriers to innovation and set themselves on the path to continual creativity. In the next chapter, we dive into the 11 main ingredients of innovation culture, before breaking down what each means and what you can do—and undo—starting tomorrow at work.

What Is Innovation Culture?

Innovation is not just about the shiny new product. Peter did not make anything new. Instead, his company innovated around the obstacles created by Covid-19. Quite often people confuse innovation with new products. While it is great to have exciting new patents, and be cranking out something new every year, innovation is more than that. Walmart innovates constantly, yet not all its innovations are obvious to its customers.[10] Innovation can be tangible or intangible and can be absent or present in

[8] "The Future of Jobs," *World Economic Forum*, January 18, 2016. www.weforum.org/reports/the-future-of-jobs.
[9] G.J. Tellis, J.C. Prabhu, R. Sethi, and K. Chandy. February 2009. "Radical Innovation Across Nations: The Preeminence of Corporate Culture," *Journal of Marketing* 73, no. 1, pp. 3–23. doi:10.1509/jmkg.73.1.3.
[10] "Innovation," Walmart. https://corporate.walmart.com/newsroom/topics/innovation.

different areas of a business. In fact, Doblin identifies 10 types of innovation pertaining to distinct aspects of a company's operation, such as innovation in core processes, brand building, or distribution channels.[11]

So, it's not just the cool kids over in product design labs or the marketing team that are solely responsible for innovation. Different companies can innovate in slightly different ways and must do so given variations in industry. For example, a formally structured manufacturing plant with bosses at the top and workers at the bottom will need to choose some different strategies compared to a team-based video game company with a flatter, more informally networked structure. However, a core convergence of factors still applies to both examples. Consequently, as we'll show, you must be "innovation ready" across the length and breadth of your organization.

We define innovation culture as a sum of the culture, systems, policies, practices, and processes in an organization that enable it to be innovative. Going back to the soup analogy, innovation culture is the soup of ingredients that enables an organization to be innovative. Our definition of innovation culture comes from a thorough review of literature, both academic and practitioner, layered with empirical findings from Sanjay's research that has led to the development of a cool tool, the InnoQ™, that you can use to see how innovative your organization currently is and, more importantly, what to do about it. For more details on InnoQ™, see Part 4 of this book.

The right culture is trajectory changing, setting the stage for continuous innovation. In fact, according to the resource-based theory that emphasizes resources and capabilities of the firm as drivers of competitive advantage, innovation culture is "a valuable organizational resource because it is created over time, is intangible, is difficult to imitate, and has the potential for moving the firm to a position of competitive advantage."[12]

A brilliant strategy without a great culture is "all hat and no cattle"— or as Peter Drucker is alleged to have pointed out, "Culture eats strategy

---

[11] "Ten Types of Innovation," Doblin. https://doblin.com/ten-types.

[12] E.J. Kleinschmidt, U. De Brentani, and S. Salomo. September 2007. "Performance of Global New Product Development Programs: A Resource-Based View," *Journal of Product Innovation Management* 24, no. 5, pp. 419–441.

for breakfast."[13] If you don't believe us, just look at some companies such as Southwest Airlines, Nordstrom, and Zappos, where leaders point to their companies' cultures as the secret of their success. Strategy is on paper, whereas culture determines how things get done. From the page to the stage, culture is comprised of the collective heart, head, and soul of an organization.

---

[13] S. Hyken. December 05, 2015. "Drucker Said 'Culture Eats Strategy For Breakfast' And Enterprise Rent-A-Car Proves It," *Forbes*. www.forbes.com/sites/ shephyken/2015/12/05/drucker-said-culture-eats-strategy-for-breakfast-and- enterprise-rent-a-car-proves-it/?sh=652b11722749.

PART 2
The Ingredients

CHAPTER 3

The Ingredient List

Extensive studies point to 11 key ingredients for this soup. Together they create innovation culture, where innovation is a habit rather than a singular event. It's culture that allows the organization to be nimble, flexible, and able to respond quickly to challenges (such as Peter's). What we present briefly here and in detail in the chapters that follow is support for these dimensions. This book shows how the dimensions work together to create a vibrant innovation culture.

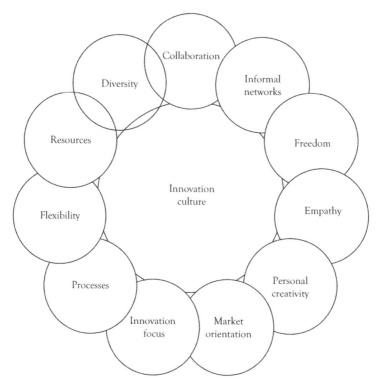

Figure 3.1 The 11 dimensions of innovation culture

If there's anything the pandemic has highlighted, it's that the importance of attending to culture will only increase exponentially for leaders at all levels. In a survey of 1,000 people managers, the Society for Human Resource Management (SHRM) found that a whopping 62 percent of HR professionals said that it had been difficult creating and sustaining workplace culture during the pandemic.[1] In a similar survey of 200 managers, McKinsey found that while a vast majority think the pandemic will change the way they do business and will have a lasting impact on their customers' needs and wants, very few (21 percent) feel they have the resources, expertise, and commitment to pursue growth over the next few years.[2]

While we discuss the 11 ingredients here briefly, each dimension is described in more detail in the chapters that follow. The ingredients come from research conducted by the first author. The research started with a thorough review of literature on the subject, both academic and practitioner. Based on this literature review, he then collected data to conduct exploratory and confirmatory research based on the data. After several iterations, he finally came up with the 11 dimensions (also part of InnoQ™, discussed later).

From a culture perspective, it's the people of an organization that drive its innovation, especially in fostering *collaboration* within and between departments. This collaboration is one of the key ingredients of innovation culture. An organization that encourages collaboration is already ahead in the game. Research has found that *informal networking* (referring to informal social connections among employees that result in more voluntary coordination than hierarchical structure) contributes to an organization's innovation readiness.[3] Informal networking works by encouraging connections within and between

[1] "The Culture Effect: Why a Positive Workplace Culture is The New Currency," *Society for Human Resource Management*. 2021. www.shrm.org/hr-today/trends-and-forecasting/research-and-surveys/documents/2021%20culture%20refresh%20report.pdf.

[2] "Innovation in a Crisis: Why it is More Critical than Ever," *McKinsey & Company*, June 17, 2020. www.mckinsey.com/business-functions/strategy-and-corporate-finance/our-insights/innovation-in-a-crisis-why-it-is-more-critical-than-ever.

[3] J.J.P. Jansen, F.A.J. Van Den Bosch, and H.W. Volberda. November 2006. "Exploratory Innovation, Exploitative Innovation, and Performance: Effects

departments and helping employees combine and develop new knowledge. Employees' *freedom* is another key component of innovation culture: empowered employees contribute to an organization's innovativeness.[4] When employees are given the freedom to think while operating in the interests of the organization, they are more likely to meaningfully work and contribute creatively to innovation.

Another important determinant of an organization's innovation culture is the level of *empathy* in the organization both internally and externally.[5] Think about it: the principles of design thinking are essentially based on empathy. With a high level of empathy for what the user is experiencing, companies can motivate creativity and innovation. To really understand a problem we are trying to solve, we must have an empathetic view of the people (customers as well as colleagues) who are experiencing that problem.

A related component is the *personal creativity* of the employees and the extent to which it is nurtured by the organization.[6] The personal creativity of the employees of the organization drives innovation. A firm's innovation can never be better than the individuals behind it—the sum of creative output comes from the interaction among a mosaic of individual, group, and organizational characteristics. Thus collaboration, informal networking, freedom, empathy, and employees' personal creativity provide a fertile ground for inter-departmental cross-pollination of ideas, enabling radically novel approaches and a truly innovative culture.

---

of Organizational Antecedents and Environmental Moderators," *Management Science* 52, no. 11, pp. 1661–1674. doi:10.1287/mnsc.1060.0576.

[4] C.B. Dobni. 2008. "Measuring Innovation Culture in Organizations: The Development of a Generalized Innovation Culture Construct Using Exploratory Factor Analysis," *European Journal of Innovation Management* 11, no. 4, p. 539. https://doi.org/10.1108/14601060810911156.

[5] B. Villari. April 2021. "The Empathic (R)evolution. Lessons Learned From Covid-19 to Design at the Community, Organization, and Governmental Levels," *Strategic Design Research Journal* 14, no: 1, pp. 187–198. doi:10.4013/sdrj.2021.141.16.

[6] A. Somech, and A. Drach-Zahavy. March 2013. "Translating Team Creativity to Innovation Implementation: The Role of Team Composition and Climate for Innovation," *Journal of Management* 39, pp. 684–708. doi:10.1177/0149206310394187.

From a systems perspective, it is important for an organization to have a *market orientation* or a deep and broad understanding of its customers, competitors, and overall markets. Extensive research has found market orientation to be essential for innovation.[7] Being connected to the customer brings new ideas from them, helping the firm convert customer needs into creative new offerings. Continuously benchmarking against competitors leads to differentiation by creating new offerings; market orientation forces employees and functional units to cooperate and collaborate in responding to market intelligence.

Together with market orientation, an organization must also have *innovation focus*—in other words, a deliberate, intentional approach toward innovation. According to the Boston Consulting Group's report on the Most Innovative Companies 2020, committed innovators win in the long run compared to skeptical or confused innovators.[8] In concrete terms, innovation focus is the extent to which the organization has formal incentives, rewards, and checkpoints for innovation.

From a process perspective, it is essential that an organization have *processes* conducive to innovation. Innovation is not occasional or in response to a specific threat. It needs to be sustained through processes that make sure innovation is a continuous part of the culture. Processes refer to specific steps that help move from ideation to production to completion and come from the merging of discipline with creative ideation—balance is key; processes should not stifle. An innate part of such nonstifling processes is the ability to pivot, change, and be nimble in processes. As such, there should be *flexibility* in an innovation culture—a bureaucratic, rule-heavy organization will find it difficult to be innovative because innovation efforts can be squelched by the stifling structure. A lack of flexibility reduces experimentation, freedom to make mistakes, and adaptive thinking.

---

[7] K. Atuahene-Gima. February 1996. "Market Orientation and Innovation," *Journal of Business Research* 35, no. 2, pp. 93–103. doi:10.1016/0148-2963(95)00051-8.

[8] M. Ringel, R. Baeza, R. Panandiker, and J.D. Harnoss. 2020. "The Serial Innovation Imperative," *Boston Consulting Group*. www.bcg.com/publications/2020/most-innovative-companies/overview.

An organization that does not set aside and direct *resources* (both human and capital) toward innovation will have a tough time building a culture that fosters it.[9] Innovation requires a continued, consistent pledge, not temporary or reactive commitments in terms of resources. Resources—both tangible (e.g., financial, tech, and equipment) and intangible (e.g., knowledge and professional development)—need to be directed specifically toward innovation.

Diversity, in information, thought, experiences, and perspectives, is important for creativity and helps an organization understand a more diverse set of customers.[10] A diverse workforce represents the diverse marketplace, helping the firm understand its consumers and their unmet market needs. Furthermore, in the creative process, diversity creates cognitive complexity: diverse people bring a diversity of thoughts, experiences, and perspectives to an organization, forcing the group to consider broader possibilities toward a wider set of solutions. A diverse group's members need to work harder and take themselves outside their comfort zone to make the results unique and creative.

Together these 11 ingredients lay the foundation for building your culture of innovation. In the next, short chapters, we turn to further details and takeaways for each ingredient. At the end of each chapter, we provide quick "what to do now" advice that you can use to kickstart your culture of innovation starting tomorrow.

---

[9] L. Wang, J.L. Jin, and D. Banister. January 2019. "Resources, State Ownership and Innovation Capability: Evidence From Chinese Automakers," *Creativity and Innovation Management* 28, no. 2, pp. 203–217. doi:10.1111/caim.12305.

[10] C.R. Østergaard, B. Timmermans, and K. Kristinsson. 2011. "Does a Different View Create Something New? The Effect of Employee Diversity on Innovation," *Research Policy* 40, no. 3, pp. 500–509. doi:10.1016/j.respol.2010.11.004.

CHAPTER 4

Cooking Together

Collaboration

"There is no special, secret sauce David," said Peter, responding to David's comment.

"Don't be modest Peter, too late for that," said David.

"What is that supposed to mean?" protested Peter.

"Just kidding dude. But on a more serious note, for one thing, your employees seem to actually love working with each other!" said David, taking a sip of his beer.

"Yours don't?"

"It's different—it's just work for them," said David. "Your peeps seem to enjoy working with each other. You guys emphasize collaboration a lot, don't you?"

"Yeah, we do," said Peter. "I read a case about Merrill Lynch in my innovation class that stuck in my head. It really brought home the importance of collaboration for me."

"I don't remember that one," said David, smiling wryly. "Maybe that's why I never emphasized collaboration." He was disappointed that his drink was all gone. "I need some more," he said before getting up. "You?"

"I am alright," said Peter.

"Be right back."

David walked back to the table with a glass. Peter and David were regular drinking buddies but, to Peter, tonight seemed different. David appeared to have an urgency about drinking that he hadn't seen before. He also wondered if there was a tinge of bitterness in David or if he was just imagining it. He wanted to help David but not at the cost of creating any tension.

"So, you were talking about Merrill Lynch," said David.

"Oh yeah," said Peter, hesitantly—he didn't want to appear preachy.

"Well, go on," said David emphatically, leaving him no choice.

Peter started describing the initiatives to increase collaboration at Merrill Lynch. At one time, most brokerages, including Merrill Lynch, had analysts who worked on their own. Across their global operations, all of the company's nearly 500 analysts worked by themselves. In fact, the star performers doubted the value of collaboration, thinking it was only for the average performers. Analysts barely knew each other. However, the times demanded a change in the culture. Investors needed collaborative research because they were not limited by geography or area of expertise. They needed integrated data on industries as they operated across the globe. The company also needed cross-sector and cross-asset research.

Within five years, under the tutelage of Candace Browning, Merrill Lynch transformed into a collaborative culture.[1] There was a concerted effort at making the culture more collaborative, including key initiatives, prodding, and rewards. Over time, the once recalcitrant researchers were spontaneously collaborating, and the result was a slew of high-quality products that differentiated the company in the industry and led to immense client satisfaction.

*   *   *

We call this the "collaboration mandate" because there is simply no way to be innovative without this core ingredient. In the 21st century, with more people coming into contact across the globe than ever before in human history, the organization that doesn't build strategies and tactics for collaboration is doomed.[2] It may seem obvious, but there is more to the value of collaboration for building a culture of innovation than meets the eye. Let's break it down a bit.

---

[1] B. Groysberg, and I. Vargas. March 2007. "Innovation and Collaboration at Merrill Lynch," *Harvard Business School*, pp. 406–081. www.hbs.edu/faculty/Pages/item.aspx?num=32914.

[2] J. Lull. 2008. *Culture-on-Demand: Communication in a Crisis World* (Malden, MA: Blackwell).

First, the days of the lone inventor are gone. No one person can have all the right answers. Additionally, once ideas are generated, many people are needed to sift and turn that data into meaningful insights. When one idea coming from one individual is built on by another, it can convert a germ of a concept into an innovative idea. Look at Aflac. When a creative team was trying to wrestle with the problem of making Aflac work, the word Aflac sounding like a duck quack came up in a creative brainstorming meeting. The rest is history.[3] This happened because the whole group worked together, building off each other.

Second, breakthrough creativity comes from "chains" of connected ideas and collaboration can speed up these chains. When individuals with diverse knowledge and skillsets work together, the confluence of their skills enhances efficiency and creativity. Even the most accomplished professionals tend to become area experts that create blind spots. The concept of "trained incapacity" gets at this idea—that the more we train ourselves into a field of thought and practice, the more we train ourselves out of all kinds of other ways of seeing and being.[4] The beauty of working with others is that it helps cover what we simply cannot perceive without others.

Finally, from a practical standpoint, "buying in" creates strength in numbers: when more people have collaborated, more people will have contributed and are likely to buy into an idea. Such ideas tend to be pushed forward further and overcome resistance more easily. This isn't a matter of opinion. Paul Nutt's work studying hundreds of organizations over decades found that the way leaders typically initiate change initiatives—through edict or by making a decision and then trying to persuade others—costs far more time and money than collaborative approaches.[5] Collaboration leads to smoother operations and less need to "put out fires

---

[3] D.P. Amos. January–February 2010. "How I Did It: Aflac's CEO Explains How He Fell for the Duck," *Harvard Business Review*. https://hbr.org/2010/01/how-i-did-it-aflacs-ceo-explains-how-he-fell-for-the-duck.

[4] K. Burke. 1984. *Permanence and Change: An Anatomy of Purpose* (Berkeley: University of California Press), p. 7, originated by Thorstein Veblen.

[5] P.C. Nutt. 2009. *Why Decisions Fail: Avoiding the Blunders and Traps That Lead to Debacles* (Oakland, CA: *Berrett-Koehler*).

on the back end," according to Jeff Dance, CEO, Fresh Consulting.[6] As an example, a focus on collaboration has led Fresh Consulting to be in the top 10 percent of ratings on company culture.[7]

J. Richard Hackman, a leading scientist studying teams, said that the right conditions for collaboration include "a compelling direction, an enabling team structure, a supportive organizational context and expert team coaching."[8] Some companies provide excellent examples. One unique way Pixar fosters collaboration is to have staff regularly share work that is not yet complete.[9] This process makes colleagues provide feedback, putting collaboration in motion. It also builds bonds between employees by showcasing their work and creative output.

Intuit does collaboration slightly differently.[10] Its employees are encouraged to move from department to department, like an exchange program (how often does this happen?) within the very organization. The objective is to bring a fresh pair of eyes and perspectives to tasks and prevent the silos that are so common to many organizations (e.g., accounting person swapping with marketing). The length of the swap depends on the manager.

Why is collaboration so hard? Aren't humans supposed to be social animals who built civilizations through teamwork? As a social species, we are hardwired to collaborate. Then why can't all humans that belong to organizations (and that's all of us) just naturally collaborate? Why does Pixar have to take deliberate steps to create collaboration and become an example for other companies to emulate?

[6] "About," Fresh Consulting. www.freshconsulting.com/about/.

[7] "Fresh Consulting," Comparably. www.comparably.com/companies/fresh-consulting.

[8] D. Hevesi. January 20, 2013. "J. Richard Hackman, an Expert in Team Dynamics, Dies at 72," *The New York Times.* www.nytimes.com/2013/01/21/business/j-richard-hackman-an-expert-in-team-dynamics-dies-at-72.html.

[9] E. Catmull. September 2009. "How Pixar Fosters Collective Creativity," *Harvard Business Review.* https://hbr.org/2008/09/how-pixar-fosters-collective-creativity.

[10] G. Abramovich. January 25, 2013. "Why Intuit Encourages Job Swaps," *Digiday.* https://digiday.com/marketing/why-intuit-encourages-job-swaps/.

Collaboration to get a fire started or hunt a wooly mammoth is different than collaboration in organizations. Organizations are complex and made of different moving parts. There needs to be collaboration within teams and between teams with different incentives and goals. That's the challenge.

*   *   *

"Collaboration often fails because of a lack of trust," said Peter.

"Trust?"

"Teams have to trust each other. I wouldn't say it's perfect, but one thing I made sure was to emphasize that right in the start. It was important to set those expectations right," said Peter.

"I can see trust within a team, why across teams?" asked David.

"When you are expecting teams to collaborate, you should not create incentives that are not aligned. You can't have one team doing well at the expense of another and expect them to collaborate. Let me give you an example. We pivoted from our core business and core customer. You know that right?"

"Yeah. You started catering to clothes manufacturers and retail," said David.

"Yeah, but if we had let only the sales and marketing team go after this segment, and not aligned manufacturing's incentives to align, they would never have worked with sales and marketing to make sure to fulfill their orders. We had to change their incentives as well to build in an incentive to pivot manufacturing lines to supply to these new customers. Collaboration involves trust. One team should trust the other team they are collaborating with, and it's on leadership to make sure incentives are aligned and teams trust each other."

"You sound like a management guru man! Why don't you start teaching a class?" said David, a bit wryly.

Given that he had pressed him for it, Peter was a little surprised at this comment but decided to remain gracious.

"Sorry, I just get a little passionate sometimes. I am no guru by any stretch, I have a lot to learn dude," said Peter.

"You do make a good point though," said David, grudgingly.

*   *   *

Gary Pisano, professor of business administration at Harvard Business School, would agree. Gary argues that organizations should balance collaboration with accountability.[11] Collaboration does not mean a lack of individual accountability by any means. Besides accountability, it is important to also have individual recognition. It is a balance. Too much emphasis on the team can lead to groupthink, especially if individual recognition is taken away. When a football team is rewarded for being a great team, the team does not cry foul if one of their ranks is declared the most valuable player (MVP). MVPs can exist in strong teams too. There is no "I" in team but there is an "e" for excellence and an "a" for achievement—those should not be stifled. Accountability, recognition, and a willingness to say "I don't know" or "I didn't get it right" are critical to trustful collaboration.

Too often collaboration can lead to groupthink, consensus, and uninspiring creativity. While collaboration requires teamwork, it is also important to recognize individual performance as well. Collaboration should never be at loggerheads with team achievement.

Key Takeaways

- Fostering collaboration is key to innovation; innovation does not tend to come from a lone genius.
- An emphasis on collaboration must come from the top.
- Create cross-functional teams composed of people with diverse skills, backgrounds, and perspectives.
- Trust is critical for collaboration; create aligned and transparent incentives among teams so that there is trust across and within teams.
- While emphasizing collaboration, also emphasize individual accountability and recognition.

---

[11] G.P. Pisano. January–February 2019. "The Hard Truth About Innovative Cultures," *Harvard Business Review.* https://hbr.org/2019/01/the-hard-truth-about-innovative-cultures.

CHAPTER 5

Mix Well

Informal Networks

As Peter and David sat enjoying their beers, a group of people walked into the bar.

"Peter!" yelled one of them, and the entire troupe walked over to their table.

"Meet my friend, David." The group was from Peter's company. A series of introductions ensued. They were all excited and in a boisterous mood. Sensing their boss and his friend were deep in serious conversation and did not want to be disturbed, after a few minutes the group decided to move to its own table.

"Nice people!" said David.

"Yeah, they are."

"Sales?"

"Actually, they are all from different departments."

"That's cool. Dad didn't encourage hallway talk. People have never really mingled that much at our company," said David ruefully.

"Just the other day, we ran into a problem," said Peter. "One of my sales guys had been asked a really tough question by a client. He just walked over to a member of the operations team, Debbie, and asked her point blank about how she'd answer it. If that had gone into the typical chain of command, Debbie would have not seen the question for a few days, let alone responded to it. That one answer saved us our relationship with the client. They would have walked away otherwise."

"He just walked over to her office?"

"Yeah."

"I mean there are no barricades in my offices either, but...," said David.

"But what?"

"My staff don't know or trust each other. Silos: my place is full of silos and politics," said David.

*   *   *

Extensive research has found that informal networking is critical for innovation.[1] Informal networks refer to informal social connections among employees that result in voluntary coordination over hierarchical structure. Work-related matters can be discussed with those who are not immediate superiors. Where informal networking is fostered, a person can feel free to talk with anyone, regardless of rank or position. Employees from different departments are comfortable networking and engaging in informal conversations with each other.

Informal networking encourages connections within and between departments.[2] It opens lines of communication. Making informal networking important also sends a message to employees that voluntary modes of coordination are important and critical, that it's okay to walk across to each other's offices—or, in remote settings, text or call someone else—and check in. Informal networking also helps employees combine and develop new knowledge, a key mechanism supporting innovation.

In the business world, the word "silos" gets thrown around a lot. We certainly hear it a lot in conversations with both clients and corporate students. Everyone recognizes silos as a negative, implying that they should not exist. But they are everywhere. Why is that?

---

[1] I. Bouty. February 2000. "Interpersonal and Interaction Influences on Informal Resource Exchanges Between R&D Researchers Across Organizational Boundaries," *The Academy of Management Journal* 43, no. 1, pp. 50–65, https://search-ebscohost-com.proxy.lib.miamioh.edu/login.aspx?direct=true&db=edsjsr&AN=edsjsr.1556385&site=eds-live&scope=site.

[2] W. Tsai. March–April 2002. "Social Structure of 'Coopetition' within a Multi-unit Organization: Coordination, Competition, and Intraorganizational Knowledge Sharing," *Organization Science* 13, no. 2, www.jstor.org/stable/3085992.

Social psychology teaches us about "ingroups versus outgroups," as part of social identity theory.[3] All of us tend to form them unconsciously. An ingroup is one in which we identify as being a member (e.g., a vegetarian might view oneself and all other vegetarians as an ingroup) whereas in an outgroup we do not identify as a member (e.g., one might view nonvegetarians as outgroups).

Without getting too much into the weeds of social identity theory, for our purposes what is important is that this categorization has mild to serious consequences. One of them is that there is ingroup favoritism—we prefer and have greater affinity for ingroup members than we do for members deemed part of outgroups. Outgroup derogation takes the idea further, where outgroup members can be seen as threatening. What is interesting is that all this goes on unconsciously—these preferences take place at the neurological level, very early on, even among infants.[4, 5]

We *all* do this unconsciously. Longstanding work on "leader–member exchange theory" highlights how, over time and without really thinking about it, leaders come to support some staff while excluding others.[6] Patterns develop, and defaults take hold that make ingroups and outgroups a constant feature of an organization's culture. What's more, the basis for identifying ingroups versus outgroups can range from the important to completely trivial and arbitrary. For example, people can form ingroups based on family, sports teams, political party, gender, religion, and more. In a famous case study, Hastorf and Cantril studied group perceptions

[3] H. Tajfel, M.G. Billig, R.P. Bundy, and C. Flament. April/June 1971. "Social Categorization and Intergroup Behavior," *European Journal of Social Psychology* 1, no. 2, pp. 149–178.

[4] A.J. Golby, J.D.E. Gabrieli, J.Y. Chiao, and J.L. Eberhardt. August 2001. "Differential Responses in the Fusiform Region to Same-Race and Other-Race Faces," *Nature Neuroscience* 4, pp. 845–850. https://doi.org/10.1038/90565.

[5] S. Sangrigoli, and S. De Schonen. August 27, 2004. "Recognition of Own-Race and Other-Race Faces by Three-Month-Old Infants," *Journal of Child Psychology and Psychiatry* 45, no. 7, pp. 1219–1227, https://doi.org/10.1111/j.1469-7610.2004.00319.x.

[6] F.C. Lunenburg. 2010. "Leader-Member Exchange Theory: Another Perspective on the Leadership Process," *International Journal of Management, Business, and Administration* 13, no. 1, pp. 1–5.

during a football game between Dartmouth and Princeton. The game, played in 1951, was a tough one, with many penalties that caused an uproar. Interestingly, when students from both universities were asked to watch the same game and respond to some questions, the students of one university "saw" the other team make over twice as many rule violations as were seen by students at the other team's university! This is evidence that we "see" and experience events that fulfill familiar patterns and with personal relevance to us.

In another famous study, researcher Tajfel found that something as trivial as preference for certain paintings can get people to form such groups within minutes.[7] Unconscious decision-making processes take place at the neurological level, where ingroup favoritism and outgroup bias occur early in perception, such as by just looking at someone's face.[8] In a way, human beings are addicted to making these types of distinctions, so we have to do all possible to break through these artificial and limiting barriers.

In a similar way, organizations have departments, teams, and, heck, even "divisions" that too easily slip into ingroups and outgroups that put up roadblocks for informal networking. Unless there is a deliberate attempt at bringing these groups together, our natural tendencies will only escalate. It does not have to be a full-blown war, but a lack of trust and cooperation can define an organization's undercurrents. During Sanjay's time in the advertising world, he saw both the negative consequences of a lack of trust and cooperation and the brilliant chemistry that resulted from connections across functional divisions. Some creative teams just worked fantastically well with account management than others. This bonhomie resulted in small, simple creative solutions that could save the day. In Don's time working in banking and broadcast radio, he too saw the ways that hierarchy can take precedence over opportunities

---

[7] H. Tajfel. November 1970. "Experiments in Intergroup Discrimination," *Scientific American* 223, no. 5, pp. 96–102, https://jstor.org/stable/24927662.

[8] K.B. Senholzi, and J.T. Kubota. 2016. "The Neural Mechanisms of Prejudice Intervention," In *Neuroimaging Personality, Social Cognition, and Character,* ed. J.R. Absher, and J. Cloutier, pp. 337–354. Academic Press. https://doi.org/10.1016/B978-0-12-800935-2.00018-X.

for innovative, informal networking. He remembers a boss who would always "get straight down to business" and never spoke with those below the fourth floor. This approach so intimidated all staff at lower levels that not only did he never learn about what was happening throughout the organization, but a culture of mini-fiefdoms and turf battles was constantly in motion. Many people in the building had worked together for years but had never even met! Informal networking aids the development of trust, cooperation, and implementation (Adler and Kwon 2002; Walker et al. 1997; Dyer and Nobeoka 2000). Without it, human beings give into the worst of their tendencies: putting up walls where none exist while failing to learn and grow.

As another anecdote closer to home, the two authors of this book sat next to each other at a conference in 2019; they started talking, grabbed some dinner and drinks, and voila, a new collaboration started! Sometimes collaboration is formed from the simplest of connections. Back to our example, a question to ask yourself is: do I/we work in Peter's company or David's? Is it somewhere in-between? You might say "Of course I know so and so. He is my son's soccer coach! He and I are in completely different teams, but we hang out and I can totally walk up to him and ask him a question." Does that count?

Individuals knowing each other by their own efforts or circumstances are great. What we're talking about is a culture in which such networking is actively encouraged at the organizational level. That takes strategic, proactive thought. For example, HubSpot encourages a "no door policy."[9] Everyone in the organization can access everyone else no matter what their position. This is different than an open-door policy where companies too often brag about their commitments to informal networking, but in the reality of day-to-day functioning, neither openness nor the building of a culture with ingredients for this soup receives any system wide attention.

Spotify similarly goes above and beyond when it comes to creating experiences that foster inclusion and connecting people. They have an entire team dedicated to creating social events to bring people together

---

[9] J. Austin. April 03, 2020. "15 Company Culture Examples That Deserve Your Attention," *Atlassian.* www.atlassian.com/blog/leadership/15-company-culture-examples-that-deserve-your-attention.

in casual settings. FitSmallBusiness is a company aimed at helping small businesses that offers a "culture committee" and "people experience specialists" who work toward creating events that promote informal networking.[10] Such events, mostly digital (and perfect for remote work), encourage employees from different time zones to get together and participate in engaging games and activities, such as "social hour."

Think of the magic Peter's company saw with that small incident when the sales member just walked up to someone on the operations team. Think of such instances happening repeatedly, as a matter of course. Not all of them may have the same impact, but over time the spirit of keeping innovation cooking is part of the culture, becoming a blueprint for practice.

Key Takeaways

- We are evolutionarily hardwired to form "ingroups" and "outgroups" (with ingroups favored and outgroups disfavored).
- Organizations need to take actions to break down such divisions across departments, divisions, teams, and so on.
- Employees spend most of their work hours with immediate colleagues (ingroup), so make sure they are making connections outside of their immediate functional groups.
- Encourage informal networking within and between different departments, divisions, and all other silos.
- Create social events in casual settings, bringing people from distinct groups together.

[10] N. Davies. October 11, 2019. "'Happiness Crews' And 'Culture Committees' Are Making Isolated Workers Feel Less Lonely," *Forbes.* www.forbes.com/sites/nigeldavies/2019/10/11/happiness-crews-and-culture-committees-are-making-isolated-workers-feel-less-lonely/?sh=1676c5df1927.

CHAPTER 6

Stir and Let Go

Freedom

"Do you all dress like this every day?" asked David, noticing that none of Peter's team, including Peter, were in formal attire.

"Pretty much."

"So, no dress code?"

"No, do you guys have one?"

"No but my dad sort of set implicit expectations and norms. We all kind of bought into it. Do you think it matters how we dress?" asked David.

"I don't think so, but it does matter if people can dress the way they want and be themselves."

"So, if I start wearing jeans to work, will I make the company more innovative?" asked David sarcastically.

"No, but over time people will feel safer, more empowered," said Peter.

*   *   *

It's not immediate or even direct, but this empowerment goes toward creating a culture. It's not just about clothes. Let people be who they are. Celebrate uniqueness. Let them celebrate their own religious or cultural events. With some minimal expectations, you've got to give people the *freedom* they deserve. From a culture perspective, *freedom* is a critical component of innovation readiness.

Empowered employees contribute to an organization's innovativeness. Freedom entails enabling ownership. If an organization treats its employees as adults and gives them the freedom to think while operating in the interests of the organization, they are more likely to meaningfully work and contribute creatively to innovation. Companies must really put their money where their mouth is; people need to feel that they have free spaces and opportunities to run with ideas, opportunities to counter dominant thinking when needed, and grow and develop.

Timothy Clark calls it "intellectual bravery."[1] Intellectual bravery is a willingness to disagree, dissent, or challenge the status quo. He laments that if there is no intellectual bravery, organizations fall into patterns. Efficiencies kill creativity, and "stagnation sets in."[2]

There is evidence that nondiscrimination laws that enable freedom cause an increase in innovation. Studying the federal Employee Non-Discrimination Act (ENDA) in the United States, Gao and Wei found that companies headquartered in states that have passed ENDAs have a significantly higher number of patents (8 percent) and patent citations (11 percent) over states that have not.[3] The differences isolated were not the result of local economic shocks or other factors like state gross domestic product (GDP), population, education, and political balance. It's no surprise then, that according to INSEAD's Global Innovation Index, democracies offering the most freedoms and protections for diverse people consistently take the lead in innovation.[4]

Dr. Shekhar Mitra and the Crest team at P&G experienced this firsthand in China.[5] The insights based on an understanding of the habits and practices of a diverse pool of respondents, including employees, led to the

---

[1] T.R. Clark. October 13, 2020. "To Foster Innovation, Cultivate a Culture of Intellectual Bravery," *Harvard Business Review.* https://hbr.org/2020/10/to-foster-innovation-cultivate-a-culture-of-intellectual-bravery.

[2] Clark. "To Foster Innovation," p. 3.

[3] H. Gao, and W. Zhang. August 17, 2016. "Non-Discrimination Laws Make U.S. States More Innovative," *Harvard Business Review*, pp. 2–4. https://hbr.org/2016/08/non-discrimination-laws-make-us-states-more-innovative.

[4] https://knowledge.insead.edu/entrepreneurship-innovation/global-innovation-index-2930.

[5] In an interview with S. Mitra, former senior vice president of Global Innovation and a member of P&G's top leadership team, the Global Leadership Council. Post retirement from P&G, he has spent seven years as a board member and strategic advisor to several F500 companies and new ventures. www.linkedin.com/in/shekhar-mitra-ph-d-4b427b47/.

creation of oral care products that were much better designed for the local consumer at a much better value.

Matt Ridley, author of several books such as *The Evolution of Everything* and *The Rational Optimist*, writes about the need for autonomy in *How Innovation Works: And Why It Flourishes in Freedom*. Ridley finds that freedom is the most important ingredient of innovation: "The main ingredient and the secret sauce that leads innovation is freedom. Freedom to exchange, experiment, imagine, invest, and fail."[6] Ridley also says that "innovation is the product of free people exchanging ideas freely" and "innovation is something that bubbles up inexorably and inevitably if you allow people the freedom to experiment and try innovative ideas." The trick with freedom, however, is to get it right.

In the organizational context, freedom is not a structureless, free-wheeling lack of instruction. While some research has looked at the control–freedom paradox (employees' freedom against organizational imperatives), recent research has found that innovators have dual motivations—both personal interest and organizational benefit.[7, 8] So, activities that are purely personally satisfying, but do not fit into the context of the organizations' needs, or vice versa, won't be enough to forge creative paths forward. Freedom and autonomy afford agency to employees by reducing the conflict or tension between an employee's personal interests and an organization's needs.

Some constraints actually flame innovation. If there were no restrictions set up, say, for product innovation at Apple, the iPhone would

---

[6] J. Pethokoukis. June 05, 2020. "Innovation, Freedom, and Prosperity: My Long-Read Q&A With Matt Ridley," *American Enterprise Institute*. www.aei .org/economics/innovation-freedom-and-prosperity-my-long-read-qa-with-matt-ridley/.

[7] T. Lempiälä, and O. Vanharanta. August 27, 2017. "Rethinking the Control–Freedom Paradox in Innovation: Toward a Multifaceted Understanding of Creative Freedom." *The Journal of Applied Behavioral Science* 54, no. 1, pp. 62–87. doi:10.1177/0021886317727458.

[8] N. Anderson, K. Potočnik, and J. Zhou. March 17, 2014. "Innovation and Creativity in Organizations: A State-of-the-Science Review, Prospective Commentary, and Guiding Framework," *Journal of Management* 40, no. 5, pp. 1297–1333. doi:10.1177/0149206314527128; J. Pfeffer. 2015. *Leadership BS: Fixing Workplaces and Careers One Truth at a Time* (New York, NY: HarperCollins).

certainly have not been as revolutionary. Yet Apple's strategy has long been to hire the best and let them be. In Steve Job's biography, Isaacson brings out this conflict: How did Steve Job's sustained oversight and management style give his employees the freedom to be innovative at the same time? While the product features and designs are part of innovation at Apple, the true innovation is much bigger than that. While restrictive parameters were set, the culture was one where freedom was valued and flourished. This again goes back to the notion that freedom does not entail a lack of boundaries or instruction. True freedom is the ability to make one's own choices and to make mistakes.

Another way to look at this is through the lens of "psychological safety": Do employees feel safe to express and be themselves? Psychological safety in organizations is the "shared belief held by members of a team that the team is safe for interpersonal risk-taking."[9] The level of openness, vulnerability, and a willingness to try something new cannot be separated from the degree to which speech and actions can take place without fear of retribution. If, for example, in a meeting two managers always dominate in bringing up ideas and initiatives, an employee may feel they're not in a safe environment for expressing themselves. The more the culture gets captured by fear (of speaking out of turn, of being wrong, of what others will do or say), the less safe everyone will feel to act freely and innovatively.

Freedom fans intrinsic motivation. It makes the act itself rewarding, without needing external pulls.[10] Innovators cherish and value this freedom from constraints, leading to more innovation. In fact, employees who are intrinsically motivated are more creative simply because their

---

[9] A. Edmondson, cited in C. Duhigg. February 25, 2016. "What Google Learned From Its Quest to Build the Perfect Team," *The New York Times Magazine*. www .nytimes.com/2016/02/28/magazine/what-google-learned-from-its-quest-to-build-the-perfect-team.html.

[10] T.M. Amabile, A. Hennessay, and B.S. Grossman. 1986. "Social Influences on Creativity: The Effects of Contracted-for Reward," *Journal of Personality & Social Psychology* 50, no. 1, pp. 14–23. doi:10.1037/0022-3514.50.1.14; C. Andriopoulos, and M. Lewis. August 2009. "Exploitation-Exploration Tensions and Organizational Ambidexterity: Managing Paradoxes of Innovation," *Organization Science* 20, no. 4, pp. 696–717. doi:10.1287/orsc.1080.0406.

efforts are more engaged and committed.[11] The crux of what's been termed "Motivation 3.0" is "autonomy," where employees relish their freedoms to think and act without fear of reprisal or being micromanaged to death.[12]

As mentioned in this book's introduction, Zappos is a company known for being extraordinarily innovative. One of the unique features of the organization is a management system dubbed "Holacracy."[13] Different than highly bureaucratic, top-down organizations, but also distinct from completely free-wheeling, anarchic systems, this flat organizational structure gives employees maximum amounts of autonomy over their work. Holacracy advocates underscore the necessity of "self-organization" (being able to make changes to improve things) and self-management (knowing exactly what one is responsible for). The main idea is to empower employees from the ground up, but to also apply just enough structure to the organization that clear pathways for decisions can be made and processes for innovation are readied and available across the company.

A sense of autonomy, instead of having to conform to an overbearing number of organizational rites, rituals, and rules, is one of the pillars of innovation that empowers employees to innovate.[14] For example, David's company did not enforce a dress code. But an implicit expectation and norm for dressing had developed. Even this subtext could make employees want to conform to these expectations, reducing feelings of safety and empowerment.[15] One client Sanjay has worked closely with is an advertis-

---

[11] T.M. Amabile. October 01, 1997. "Motivating Creativity in Organizations: On Doing What You Love and Loving What You Do," *California Management Review* 40, no. 1, pp. 39–58. doi:10.2307/41165921.

[12] "Pink's Autonomy, Mastery and Purpose Framework," Mindtools. n.d. www.mindtools.com/pages/article/autonomy-mastery-purpose.htm.

[13] "Holacracy and Self-Organization," Zappos Insights. 2022. www.zapposinsights.com/about/holacracy. This is based on the book by B.J. Robertson. 2015. *Holacracy: The New Management System for a Rapidly Changing World* (New York, NY: Henry Holt).

[14] E. Shook, and J. Sweet. 2019. "Getting to Equal 2019: Creating a Culture That Drives Innovation," *Accenture*. www.accenture.com/us-en/about/inclusion-diversity/gender-equality-innovation-research.

[15] For more on what Sostrin calls "the hidden curriculum" always operating in any organization, see the chapter "Re-Making Communication: The Competitive

ing agency that not only allows employees to be the way they'd like to be, but also provides for an excellent work–life balance through flexible work arrangements. This employee offering has been further supported during Covid through an emphasis on work from home. Employees have more time to play with their kids, take an afternoon off to go to the doctors or get shopping done, or even connect with a friend over coffee. While this particular agency enjoys the pleasures of working from home, even the employees realize that there needs to be some face time as well— so they will be moving to a three days at the office two days at home, hybrid format.

Once clarity of purpose and some minimal expectations are set forth, without ambiguity, the rest can be left to the freedom of the employees. When an employee feels safe and empowered, the benefits of freedom should immediately start showing in their productivity, motivation, and drive. These are intangibles worth investing in.

Key Takeaways

- If an organization treats its employees well, giving them the freedom to think and operate in the interests of the organization, they are more likely to work toward its interests and contribute creatively to innovation.
- Provide employees with safe spaces (such as lounges separate from workspaces to have private conversations or opportunities for anonymous feedback on company policies), and empower them with a sense of freedom that they not only can do requested work, but have time to work on their own, generated projects).
- Freedom does not mean a lack of instruction. Provide overall guardrails and structures, but let employees have freedom within those boundaries.

Advantage of the Twenty-First Century," in J. Sostrin. 2013. *Re-Making Communication at Work* (New York, NY: Palgrave Macmillan), pp. 61–64.

- Provide as much flexibility as possible in work arrangements and means of getting tasks done (e.g., flexible work from home policies).

CHAPTER 7

Let Seep

Empathy

"Are you OK?" said Peter, looking at David intently. He noticed that David had suddenly become silent.

David briefly flinched but the typical bravado he had used all through his life clouded this response as well.

"I am doing great! Why do you ask?"

"I know you," said Peter. There was a pause.

"It does suck man. Honestly. Firing people is not easy."

"Good to hear that honesty from you," said Peter.

"What good is it now?" asked David.

"It is a good sign. It shows you care."

"You thought I didn't?" asked David.

"Well, frankly, I have not seen this side of you before. You were always about bottom lines, costs, and the rest. I hate to put it this way, but to be real with you, I guess it took firing a few people before you felt for them."

"My people like me!" said David.

"Of course, they do," said Peter.

"Correction, they liked me until Covid happened," said David with a chuckle.

"I didn't mean to say they don't like you," said Peter.

"I know. I was just giving you a hard time, Peter. I think I am also a little bit bitter today," said David.

"Seems like you feel really bad for letting your employees go," said Peter.

"Phil has a family, three kids with growing needs. You're right. I feel for him man. I could also kind of empathize—since Covid, there have been many times I have doubted if I will get a paycheck," said David.

*   *   *

Ah, empathy! Quite the pervasive buzzword nowadays, isn't it? However, if we underappreciate and don't have a plan for implementing empathy, the results will be devastating. Ask anyone what empathy means and the answer will often be "an ability to put yourself in another's shoes." Yeah, yeah, we all get it. Or do we?

Let's see, what is empathy? Empathy is the ability to understand someone else's feelings and perspectives and understand their point of view alongside them. Empathy involves intellectual identification with the other. It also involves a sense of vicarious experience, a mirroring of others' opinions, hopes, and pain points. It involves the mind, body, spirit, and attention to the details of others' inner and outer contexts.[1] To really get empathy, you must engage in what improvisers call "whole body listening" to all the complex dimensions that make up every single person on earth.

Empathy is not pity, or sympathy. Feeling bad for your colleague who just had a tough quarter, a client call, or day at home is not empathy. It's more than that. It reflects an attempt to simulate the experience of your colleagues' situations and an attempt, however incomplete, to perceive their emotional and mental experiences with humility and without judgment. It's like a method actor who delves into experiences from her own life to get closer to what her character is experiencing. The empaths are not detached. Instead, they are active, respectful, and curious.

Okay, that's fine, all sounds great. But how might empathy influence innovation? Extensive research, including Sanjay's own, has found empathy to be highly predictive of a company's innovativeness. The principles of design thinking are essentially based on empathy. With a high level of empathy for what the user is experiencing, companies can motivate

---

[1] For more on this view, see D. Waisanen. 2021. *Leadership Standpoints* (New York, NY: Cambridge University Press).

creativity and innovation. In fact, many fields are waking up to the idea that their best path forward involves a cocreative rather than top-down approach to innovation.[2] To really understand a problem we are trying to solve, we must have an empathetic view of the people (customers/clients and colleagues) who are experiencing that problem. Empathy means understanding what's important to people and understanding their struggles.

We see this on a regular basis in design thinking and innovation workshops with corporate groups. In fact, we deliberately insert a "nonempathetic" condition in these workshops to make a point. Participants are asked to design a product (e.g., a wallet or retail environment) without first speaking or engaging with their priority audience. Mind you, a lot of these groups consist of people who work in class together for a while and know each other. Yet, the products they come up with for this group of people tend to be typically off-base. They exhibit weaknesses in what "we think we know"—group members often tend to project what they think the person would want, not what they really want, based on a lack of empathetic understanding of that person. In the condition that introduces a chance for the group to engage empathetically, there is a distinct difference in the solutions.

Intuit's design for delight is a perfect example.[3] It focuses on a deep empathy of the company's consumers. While Intuit has different terminology, the company is following the steps of design thinking—use divergent (where ideas are generated) and convergent (where ideas are sifted and edited) thinking followed by rapid experimentation. The "deep empathy" comes not from surveys or focus groups but from what they call "follow me homes" in which customers are observed at home or work, in their natural habitats, without any questions or probing. Intuit aims to gather a deep understanding of their pain points and needs. It's what been dubbed "thick description" or "thick culture," following the work of anthropologists going into situations and seeking to understand the meanings people create in real-life situations—instead of presuming to

---

[2] C.H. Botan. 2017. *Strategic Communication Theory and Practice: The Cocreational Model* (Hoboken, NJ: Wiley).

[3] "Design for Delight," Intuit Labs, www.intuitlabs.com/design-for-delight.

know anything about anyone else with advance labels and judgments.[4] These observations lead to inputs that form the basis of rapid prototyping and experimentation in a quest to find solutions to pain points and needs.

The role of empathy in innovation is underscored by the simple observation that *innovation is, by its very nature, a result of someone's frustration or dissatisfaction with the current.* Whether it was Steve Job's displeasure at not being able to carry his music in his pocket or the emergence of ride-sharing companies like Uber due to the unhappiness of its founders with the dominance of traditional taxi services, such examples all share the same grounding in moments of "I wish the world wasn't this way."

Microsoft CEO Satya Nadella says, "Empathy makes you a better innovator. If I look at the most successful products, we [at Microsoft] have created, it comes with that ability to *meet the unmet, unarticulated needs of customers.*"[5] Nadella should know. When he was 29, his son Zain was born with cerebral palsy. He has gone on record to ask, "Why did this happen to me?" His experience with a special needs child sparked his interest in accessibility that is now a key focus for Microsoft. Windows 10 has new capabilities involving an eye gaze function that's useful for Amyotrophic Lateral Sclerosis (ALS) sufferers. Microsoft learning tools help people with reading and writing challenges (e.g., dyslexia), letting them read content aloud, break words into syllables, adjust text size, and background color.[6]

None of this attention to client needs might have been possible without Nadella being forced into a world where people like his son confront the challenges of digital life. So, one additional benefit of empathy is that it makes one pay attention to needs for more inclusivity. From a business perspective, there's a compelling case that failing to push one's

---

[4] See C. Geertz. 2008. *Thick Description: Toward an Interpretive Theory of Culture* (New York, NY: Routledge).

[5] Emphasis added. "3 CEOs Using Empathy to Unlock Innovation," *Twenty One Toys.* 2021. https://twentyonetoys.com/blogs/future-of-work/3-ceos-using-empathy-to-unlock-innovation.

[6] "Microsoft CEO S. Nadella: How Empathy Sparks Innovation," *Knowledge@Wharton.* February 22, 2018. https://knowledge.wharton.upenn.edu/article/microsofts-ceo-on-how-empathy-sparks-innovation/.

perspectives outward (what improvisers often call "external focus") will lead to not only falling sales but decreased legitimacy in a world where diverse people rightfully claim, and expect, to be heard.

Empathy need not be just outward, or customer focused, though. A truly innovative organization is empathetic toward its employees. Zoom is a perfect example. Due to a worldwide pandemic, Zoom has managed to make its way into most homes and offices. Besides its technical prowess, the company is also well known for the amount it cares for its people. If you visit Zoom's blog, you will see an eclectic collection of entries from several employees documenting their struggles and sharing how the company culture emphasizes "we are all in this together"—that it cares.[7] For instance, Zoom encourages employees across departments to "babywear" during meetings or take time during the working day to help kids with school, supporting working parents and caregivers. CEO Eric Yuan describes the Zoom mission simply as "deliver happiness."

Just like Peter's company, Zoom has adapted to the pandemic. Nearly a third of its new employees never set foot in the office or have met their manager or teammates in person.[8] What this has entailed is a special effort to keep employee morale high. And this isn't just some whimsical preference—research has now made abundantly clear how superior remote work can be for productivity and many of the ingredients described in this book when leaders are strategic and get the recipe for such success right.[9] This is probably why Zoom came up with a "happiness crew," a team whose focus is to keep employees happy as the company grows. Zoom also offers training sessions, mentorship, and volunteering opportunities to keep the employees happy.

True empathy begins before any extreme event like firing. It's proactive rather than reactive. Much like Zoom, if David had invested in his employees' happiness, he may not have faced a situation like this. He is

---

[7] "Blog," Zoom. https://blog.zoom.us/.

[8] D. Howley. December 10, 2020. "A 'Happy Crew' and Unlimited Vacation: What It's Like Working at Zoom," *Yahoo Finance*. https://finance.yahoo.com/news/what-its-like-working-at-zoom-142628732.html.

[9] T. Neeley. 2021. *Remote Work Revolution: Succeeding from Anywhere* (New York, NY: Harper Business).

confronted with a critical question, in this regard: just why is it so hard to be empathetic while someone is in your organization and feel terrible when they have left? And how can one nip this threshold of pain in the bud before it gets crossed? Indeed, as illustrated in this conversation, empathy has boundary conditions.

There is an underlying pathos in the previous scene. David is clearly hurting but, at the same time, he has often perceived himself (and thinks others perceive him) as perfect, the guy for whom nothing could go wrong. Yet, after the experience of needing to let employees go, he knew exactly what Peter was referring to.

Almost as if a button had been pushed, David could see it clearer than daylight that his practices had been remiss. Yet he had let it pass, just never having the gumption to break the inertia. He had heard about things like empathy and the need to empathize with customers and employees. He had read about it, just never acted on it. And that's the critical part here: it's what one does to achieve empathy that most matters.

Key Takeaways

- Empathy drives innovation—empathy with customers provides inspiration for creativity and innovation.
- Be user-centric: think of the customer, their pain points, and their situations in life; listen closely and expect to be surprised.
- Be ready to prototype and experiment in providing solutions to the customer.
- Be empathetic to employees and their own life situations— happy employees who feel heard and valued are productive and innovative.

CHAPTER 8

Sprinkle in Inspiration

Personal Creativity

"It's interesting," said David.

"What?"

"You know, just comparing your company against mine."

Peter was increasingly aware of what David had been doing all evening, while consuming copious amounts of alcohol.

"I noticed you are doing that," said Peter. "Don't you think that's a bit presumptuous and simplistic?"

"What do you mean?"

"I mean you are trying to connect how my team goes out to drink and dresses to how well my company is doing. Surely there is more to running a business than that."

"It's just a reflection Peter, a reflection of the cultures. That's what I am noting," said David. "It's just an interesting window into the soul of our companies."

Peter understood what David was saying. Part of him was also finding this comparison interesting but he was also mindful of the tough times David was going through. He had always noticed the differences in their cultures. He believed passionately in the importance of culture and getting the elements of culture. He had invested time, money, and energy making sure of that. Believing that his approach was the right one, he secretly hoped David would learn something, but he also wanted to be sensitive to his state of mind.

"I feel like some of the things we talked about can definitely help in creativity," said David.

"Yeah, there is a ton of research on the importance of creating the right environment for employee creativity to flourish," said Peter.

*   *   *

Like the tiny cells of a mosaic that work together to paint a picture, the personal creativity of an organization's employees drives innovation. A firm's innovation can never be better than the individuals behind it. While synergies can lead to the whole being greater than the sum of the parts, what's not often recognized in work on innovation is how much the whole cannot exist without its parts. This means that companies need people committed to creativity to innovate. Indeed, companies such as Google, Pixar, and Apple have shown that they can increase their organizational creativity by building environments for their employees' individual creativity to shine.

In general, researchers have identified *creativity* as broadly centering on *idea generation* whereas *innovation* emphasizes *implementation*, implying that creativity is the first step toward innovation. Researchers have used the interactionist perspective to formalize the relationship between innovation and individual creativity.[1] This perspective believes that creativity arises out of a complex interaction between the individual and their work situation.

At the individual level, personal creativity is the result of individual characteristics and circumstances (such as cognitive style, ability, personality, knowledge, motivation, social influences, and physical environment). At the team level, creativity arises out of the interaction between personal and group characteristics, such as group norms, processes, and culture. At the organizational level, innovation is a function of both individual and group creativity. The gestalt of creative output (new products, services, ideas, procedures, and processes) emanates from the interaction among a complex mosaic of individual, group, and organizational characteristics.

---

[1] R.W. Woodman, J.E. Sawyer, and R.W. Griffin. April 1993. "Toward a Theory of Organizational Creativity," *The Academy of Management Review* 18, no. 2, pp. 293–321. https://jstor.org/stable/258761.

Let's look at a simple example. The first author had a student who worked at a production facility for a beer company. He often complained about inefficiencies and incompetence at the assembly line. One day, he just decided to give some improv games he had learned in class a try with his team. He got them together, ran the games, and found success—his team took to the games. They created more cohesive groups, better teamwork, and fewer inefficiencies. The student could have taken one of two choices. He could either continue toeing the line, executing, and staying true to a routine and habits clearly leading to unwanted outcomes. Or he could commit to trying something creative and new. Where did the idea come from? Definitely not from his employer, as he had been doing the same thing for years! It came from inspiration, from trying out some improv exercises he had learned in class, which he had fun doing with his classmates.

If David's company had encouraged creative endeavors at the individual level, this would have been one part of the engine for innovation at the organizational level. Instead, the culture at David's organization was one of execution, habit, and routine—attending neither to the means nor the ends of innovation.

Unfortunately, many times, we hear employees complain of feeling like a "cog in the wheel"—their creative talents insufficiently used, they feel utterly helpless. As the interactionist perspective argues, organizational creativity comes from a complex interaction between the components. If employees do not feel creative, they'll leave the mosaic incomplete. Thus, how creative an individual employee thinks and feels is a predictor of an organization's innovativeness (see Part 4, Chapter 2 for more on this).

Companies can invest resources in creating systems, research and development laboratories, and other infrastructure aimed at innovation. However, if they are unable to provide the environment for the creativity of their employees to flourish, there can be no innovation. There is simply no way that an organization can begin on a journey toward innovation if its people do not feel creative. So how can they do this?

Well, there's the extreme version. Listen to what Ben Chestnut, cofounder and CEO of Mailchimp, thought about personal creativity: "So later in life, I start my company and that's how I run it. I only hire weirdos, basically, and I just let them fail all the time. It just makes perfect sense to me."[2] Mailchimp has done extraordinary work in creating a creative corporate culture—from the development of Mailchimp University to the creation of a different kind of CCO, the chief culture officer. To strengthen and not just maintain their creative culture, they also have an extensive onboarding program for new hires called "Chimpanion."[3]

From another angle, Google founders Larry Page and Sergey Bring wrote the "20 percent project" into their initial public offering letter. This project encourages employees to spend 20 percent of their time working on what they, on an individual level, think would benefit Google the most and help it in its quest for innovation. That's really putting one's money where their mouth is—talk about encouraging personal creativity!

Wistia encourages employees to get involved in outside projects. IBM offers InnovationJam, a platform for online collaboration to help organizations unleash their employees' creativity.[4] Amazon taps into the creativity of its employees through its "working backwards" program, where employees are encouraged to submit their plans that include customer impact, mock press release, questions, and reactions from different business areas. In fact, the Prime Now and Amazon Smile programs started due to this initiative.[5] Procter & Gamble organizes regular and periodic Lighthouse innovation exercises dedicated to a specific category or brand or new business development.

The body language of clients often shows how they are taken aback at some of these notions. Sanjay had two clients who looked at each other and opined that all the above sounded like ultra-liberal, corporate fads, that nothing about personal creativity should be a top priority for their bottom line focused company. Let's set aside, for a moment, their lack of awareness of, for instance, how a survey of 349 executives from across the

[2] As cited in Zapier's blog. D. Schreiber. April 08, 2014. "The Secret Behind MailChimp's Creative Culture, Even As It Grows," *Zapier*. https://zapier.com/blog/mailchimp-creative-company/.

[3] "Maintaining Company Culture Through Onboarding," *MailChimp*. September 29, 2015. https://mailchimp.com/culture/maintaining-company-culture-through-onboarding/.

[4] "Home Page," InnovationJam. www.collaborationjam.com/.

[5] Fast Company. August 05, 2019. "The 50 Best Workplaces for Innovators," *Fast Company*. www.fastcompany.com/best-workplaces-for-innovators/2019.

world showed that 90 percent identified "organizational agility" as a key differentiator in their current environment, or even how 1,500 chief executives from 60 countries highlighted "creativity" as the most important skill for future leaders and organizations.[6, 7] The general vibe with Sanjay's clients was that they had more important fish to fry. That it's okay for the big guys with deep pockets to do all these fancy things, but there was no value in it for an organization such as theirs. Some of you reading this book might be nodding your head in agreement: it sounds and rings true, right? And we certainly get it. There's a longstanding assumption that there are "hard skills" of business and then the "soft skills" of everything else that's just the icing on the cake. But this is a premise that has outlived its usefulness. As research has made abundantly clear, the value to the bottom line of "intangible assets" is greater than ever. And according to some calculations, even surpasses the value of tangible assets in many cases.[8] The question becomes one of priority. Is this something a company should prioritize and invest in? The answer for innovation, based on deep and broad evidence, is a resounding yes! Think about it a little differently. Why do people invest in a quality education for their children? It's an investment that will shape thinking, which will shape their futures.

One qualification is in order with the development of personal creativity. There is considerable research showing that intrinsic motivation is helpful while extrinsic motivation can be detrimental to creativity. What does all this mean? If employees are motivated intrinsically, for example, by passion for the work itself rather than by extrinsic rewards, they are likely to be more creative and work harder. When employees are excited

---

[6] Economist Intelligence Unit. March 2009. "Organisational Agility: How Business Can Survive and Thrive in Turbulent Times," *Economist*. www.emc.com/collateral/leadership/organisational-agility-230309.pdf.

[7] "IBM 2010 Global CEO Study: Creativity Selected as Most Crucial Factor for Future Success," *IBM*. May 18, 2010. www.ibm.com/news/ca/en/2010/05/20/v384864m81427w34.html.

[8] See M.W. Ragas, and R. Culp. 2014. *Business Essentials for Strategic Communicators: Creating Shared Value for the Organization and its Stakeholders* (New York, NY: Palgrave Macmillan); M.J. Canel, and V. Luoma-aho. 2018. *Public Sector Communication: Closing Gaps Between Citizens and Public Organizations* (Hoboken, NJ: Wiley).

about the work and the tasks they perform, they tend to be far more likely to explore innovative approaches, play with different ideas, use divergent thinking, and concentrate on the tasks for a longer period.

Considering what we've learned about personal creativity, should David try to make his employees feel creative by motivating them intrinsically or throw money at them as an incentive (extrinsic motivation)? While task completion itself may increase in the case of monetary rewards, creativity itself may not. If creativity is valued, then creating a culture conducive to creativity through, for example, transformational leadership will have a better impact than only monetary reward. If you create a culture that emphasizes employee creativity, no one will feel like a cog in the wheel, and no one will dial in the work. One creative event will lead to another and then another. And over time, the cumulative effect of individual creative events will drive organizational innovation.

Key Takeaways

- Organizational creativity comes from a complex interaction. If employees do not feel creative, organizational innovation will be hampered. In other words, how creative individual employees think they are reflects, and is a predictor of, an organization's innovativeness.
- When employees are excited about the work and the tasks that they perform for their own sake, they are far more likely to explore innovative approaches.
- As opposed to being constantly told what to do, allow employees time to pursue their own project that they think will make the company more innovative.
- Intrinsic motivation may be better able to encourage creativity than extrinsic motivation.
- Reward and recognize individual creativity through organizational emails and events.

CHAPTER 9

Look Outside

Market Orientation

"I am starting to get hungry," said David.

"They have a food truck now!" said Peter.

"They do? Since when?"

"Been a few days. I was talking to the owner," said Peter. "Apparently he heard his 'customers' voice'——they had been asking for food."

"Cool!"

"Yeah, Lorenzo runs the truck. He is a gourmet chef who does this on the side. He likes experimenting with flavors and sort of uses this as a testing ground. Last time I was here, he had Tacos with a French twist. Killer," said Peter.

"What are we waiting for? Let's go!"

David led the way as they both got up, looking for the food truck.

"He is out in the back, kind of tucked away behind those trees. Ah! There he is."

*   *   *

The best cooks never stick with the same old recipe. Although restaurants have their greatest hits that will keep customers coming back, time after time, it's the truly innovative chefs who look to what others are doing, travel to other places, and try to find new combinations of ingredients that will be the next big dish. If there's one message of this chapter, it is *get out of the kitchen*. For innovation to truly work, every employee at an organization must simply look and search outward. Innovators focus externally as inspiration for new ideas.

We've got to keep our ears and eyes to the ground to innovate well. No company exists in a vacuum. All firms operate in an environment replete with competition to serve their customers. Market orientation refers to the extent to which a firm understands its customers, its markets, and its competition. In that sense, market orientation is an element of organizational culture that reflects how its employees think and act as a marketing organization. The ability to sense the market, feel out the competition, understand the customer, and provide customer service are key ingredients of a firm's market orientation. And the ties with empathy here shouldn't be lost. Quite simply, innovation can be about compassionate reaction as much as action.

In a famous paper, Kohli and Jaworski (1990) define market orientation as consisting of three elements: collecting, disseminating, and responding to intelligence (customers, competition, and markets). In that sense, market orientation is a philosophy and approach to business. The first step is the collection of intelligence, both formal and informal. To Kohli and Jaworski, this step is not just the sole preserve of the marketing department but of the entire organization—whether it is R&D executives coming back from conferences or senior manufacturing executives coming back from trade conferences with intelligence, and so on. Once collected, the organization needs to make this intelligence available within the organization and then respond to it. It is not just enough to collect intelligence; it must be distributed to everyone with an expectation that they can and should respond to it. Nearly all departments within a company need to know this critical dimension.

The link between market orientation and innovation is incredibly strong. Market orientation drives innovation and there are essentially three reasons why. First, understanding and being connected to the customer brings new ideas from the marketplace and other environments, helping the firm to be more innovative by identifying and converting customer needs into creative product ideas and new offerings. Second, a market-oriented firm continuously benchmarks against competitors by following, analyzing, and responding to competitors' moves. This leads to a need for and ability to differentiate an organization from the competition by creating new offerings.

Finally, a market orientation forces employees and functional units of the firm to cooperate and collaborate to respond to market intelligence.

This increased communication and integration creates a more open and receptive organizational climate that is conducive to innovation than those sticking with old habits. Employees in a market-oriented firm also tend to be incentivized for taking risks in generating creative ideas.

In fact, market orientation has also been found to be an important precursor to innovation. Let's look at some recent examples, such as Nike. "Stuck indoors and need a sweat? We've got your back," it says on Nike's website. During the pandemic, Nike heard its customers' needs and wants and made free training videos on YouTube and its Training Club app free. As a result, it acquired a whopping 25 million new members and saw an 83 percent increase in its digital sales. (as reported in Nike News). In essence,

> NIKE's strong results this quarter and full fiscal year demonstrate its unique competitive advantage and deep connection with consumers all over the world. FY21 was a pivotal year for NIKE as they brought their Consumer Direct Acceleration strategy to life across the marketplace. "Fueled by our momentum, we continue to invest in innovation and our digital leadership to set the foundation for NIKE's long-term growth." (John Donahoe, president and CEO of the company).[1]

During the pandemic, when shoppers started keeping away from brick-and-mortar stores, Shopify also stepped up its game by offering tools to help retailers convert their points-of-sale terminals into e-commerce stores. Both examples of innovation were driven by being closely in touch with customers. Amazon has shown the world what being focused on the customer and being market oriented in general can do to the fortunes of a company. Whatever you think of Jeff Bezos, his focus on market orientation cannot be ignored. As quoted in an interview to the *Wall Street Journal*, Bezos said, "The [number] 1 thing that has made us successful by far

---

[1] "Nike, Inc. Reports Fiscal 2021 Fourth Quarter and Full Year Results," *Nike News*, June 24, 2021. https://news.nike.com/news/nike-inc-reports-fiscal-2021-fourth-quarter-and-full-year-results.

is obsessive compulsive focus on the customer."[2] Bezos believes that the only way to growth is through customer preoccupation, criticizing other companies who reverse this equation by prioritizing their competition. Phil Knight, the CEO of Nike, was also quoted in the *Harvard Business Review* as saying, "while technology is still important, the consumer has to lead innovation."[3]

Coca-Cola is another famous company known for its market orientation. While it does an incredible amount of research on consumer tastes and preferences, including studies and development on new tastes and formulations, the company also has its ear to the ground in terms of the overall market. Its strategic acquisition of brands such as Dasani, Honest Tea, Smartwater, Simply Orange, Minute Maid, and Vitaminwater are all products oriented toward satisfying changing, health-conscious desires among consumers.

As Covid has ravaged economies and put many organizations out of business, or just led to significant challenges, some have used their market orientation to innovate. One simple example is how some restaurants have responded to Covid. Katz is a famous Deli based out of New York City. It is featured in many a Hollywood film, documentaries, and food shows. In a practice that could never have been envisioned even a decade ago, Katz is now offering shipping of their signature meats, breads, cheeses, and condiments to every part of the United States! The company's intelligence has told Katz that not only is there a demand for its food across the country, but also that a lot of people are leaving NYC but feel nostalgic and miss the flavors and smells of the city—hence the digital operation now makes perfect sense. In sensing the new market orientations afoot, Katz has become truly innovative during a period of incredible hardship.

What about in other countries? Does a market orientation work the same way across the world? In Columbia, companies have traditionally only

---

[2] L. Stevens. September 14, 2018. "Leadership and Life Lessons from Amazon's Jeff Bezos," *The Wall Street Journal.* www.wsj.com/articles/leadership-and-life-lessons-from-jeff-bezos-1536938179.

[3] G.E. Willigan. July–August 1992. "High-Performance Marketing: An Interview With Nike's Phil Knight," *Harvard Business Review.* https://hbr.org/1992/07/high-performance-marketing-an-interview-with-nikes-phil-knight.

focused on rationalization, cost cutting, and quality. Wilches, Valencia, and Jimenez set out to study the relationship between market orientation and innovation in the country.[4] They conducted an extensive survey among directors with a global vision as part of their responsibilities in 77 Colombian companies. As hypothesized, they found convincing evidence for a market orientation to predict innovation (in this case, product innovation). In another study in Australia, the renowned expert on marketing orientation, Kwaku Atuahene-Gima investigated 275 companies (158 manufacturing, 117 services) and found market orientation also strongly drives innovation in that society.

There are countless other examples of how companies tuned in to their customers, markets, and competitors to translate insights into innovation. A strong market orientation facilitates innovation by providing a culture that enhances creativity, risk taking, and an ability to identify novel opportunities.

The message is clear—be tuned in! Market orientation can be enforced through a formal programmatic commitment to a process-driven approach of collecting, disseminating, and responding to market intelligence. It can be nurtured as a pervasive aspect of the company's culture through statements, onboarding, and more, but is best when aligned with on-the-ground, ongoing commitments that embed the orientation among all employees within. However expressed, no innovation is possible without a market orientation.

*   *   *

"You know something you said made me think," said David as they walked back to their table, having placed their orders.

"What?"

"He heard the customers' voice."

"Oh yeah. Everyone has to, no matter what industry," said Peter.

---

[4] A.C. Ocampo Wilches, J.C. Naranjo Valencia, and D.J. Jiménez. June 01, 2016. "Market Orientation and Innovation: Do Structure and Environment Moderate This Relationship?" *Revista ESPACIOS* 39, no. 42. www.revistae spacios.com/a18v39n42/a18v39n42p09.pdf.

"Well…"

"Oh, come on! Don't say 'my dad never believed in that'! That's just basic business wisdom man."

Peter was starting to feel as if David had got into a state of mind where he was just apportioning blame, not taking responsibility.

"Yes and no," said David.

"Meaning. . . ?"

"It's the difference between lip service and a deliberate, intentional approach toward what you call market orientation," said David.

"Dude. Sorry to say, but it's easy to say, 'Dad screwed up.'"

"I know. I should have changed things."

"It's never too late; it's not like you are shutting down," said Peter. "I think I might have something that could help you."

Key Takeaways

- Understanding and being connected to the customer brings new ideas to the marketplace, helping a firm be more innovative by identifying and converting needs into creative product ideas and new offerings.
- Continuously benchmarking against competitors by following, analyzing, and responding to their moves leads to an ability to differentiate oneself by creating new offerings and innovating.
- A market orientation forces employees and functional units of the firm to cooperate and collaborate to respond to market intelligence.
- Trend-based intelligence, mapping emerging or better competitor products, can lead to new products more cost effectively than developing from scratch.
- Be tuned in to customer, competitors, and markets, both formally and informally.

CHAPTER 10

The Heart of the Soup

Innovation Focus

The buzzer from the food truck went off on the table, signaling that their food orders were ready. Peter and David looked at it with excitement.

"Looks like it is ready my friend," said David, rubbing his hands with glee as he got up.

"Yeah, let's go! Can't wait to try those Korean style sliders!"

They came back a few minutes later, carrying their food.

"Amazing!" said David, taking a satisfying bite of his slider.

"Lorenzo is a genius," said Peter with a mouthful.

"Man, the flavors are really good!"

For the first time in the evening, both men were quiet as they enjoyed the sliders; they desisted from all conversation out of respect for the food.

"I am glad we did this today, Peter," said David.

"So am I!"

"You know, you are probably the best person I could have met today."

"My pleasure!"

"I have always sort of thought about how your company feels different but today I am really starting to see it more clearly," said David.

"Why is that?"

"I don't know. I think I really liked Phil and the meeting today with him jolted me," said David.

"Phil is the guy you fired a few minutes ago?"

"Yeah," said David. "Sometimes you need a kick in the pants; I got mine today."

"Well, I am glad if it is helping."

"Well, I think it's also that I am talking to you. I always admired the way you ran things and today I am just breaking it down a little bit," said David. "I had never truly grasped the importance of innovation before."

"Innovation isn't some mysterious force man," said Peter. "To my mind, it's just the result of creating the right culture. Don't get me wrong, you must plan for and see innovation deliberately. You also have to focus on it whole heartedly but the way to actually achieve it is through culture."

"Focus on innovation," said David smiling, "I don't know how many times I heard that phrase during my MBA days."

"It's true. It's about constantly creating a dialogue that centers the importance of innovation," said Peter.

"How did you do that?"

"I think I was focused on it and that just permeated. We did have a lot of processes and systems for it, but we also kept it *salient* in people's minds. It was this thing that was in the air. That's where some of the seemingly 'fluffy' things help."

"You mean the ping pong tables and bring your dogs to work culture?" asked David.

"Yeah. I personally think that ping pong doesn't necessarily lead to a brilliant idea, but I think it keeps emphasizing a certain set of messages unconsciously."

"I think I have far more important priorities and use of my money than installing ping pong tables in my offices, man!" said David.

"Okay, you asked me, that's why I am telling you. It looks like a waste of money now but it's a sound investment in your innovation culture. By that I don't mean just ping pong tables—I am using them as metaphors only. You don't need ping pong tables specifically. You just need tangible and intangible supports for priming the pump, creating that culture of innovation, and emphasizing to your team that you focus—consciously—on innovation," said Peter.

*   *   *

An important part of innovation culture is keeping everyone attending to innovation itself. In more concrete terms, innovation focus is the extent to which the organization has formal incentives, rewards, and checkpoints or signposts for innovation—in other words, a deliberate, intentional approach toward innovation. To be clear, these can certainly be extrinsic motivators (such as rewards or incentives) or intrinsic motivation (such as personal fulfillment) to flourish. An innovation focus doesn't replace or act in isolation from all that has preceded this chapter, but sweetens, or in our case, salts, the pot.

Now, isn't it a bit obvious that, to be good at something, one needs to focus on it? That's why we emphasize the metaphor of shaking the salt here. When creating the soup, it's easy to forget that one of the central ingredients needs a dash of attention itself. We've both heard soup makers say, "this soup needs more salt" or "this soup is too salty." Similarly, you need just enough attention to innovation to keep everyone's sights set on the goal, but not so much that it becomes overbearing or crowds out the importance of all the other ingredients.

There is no doubt that an innovation focus is important. The more important question is how this effort is defined and quantified. A firm can be said to be focused on innovation if it has formal practices and standards in place to incentivize innovation.

The Boston Consulting Group (BCG) has been tracking the 50 most innovative companies since 2005.[1] Of the 162 companies it has tracked, only 8 have repeatedly made the list (Alphabet, Amazon, Apple, HP, IBM, Microsoft, Samsung, and Toyota). BCG classifies companies into three categories: "committed" innovators (45 percent) are those that not only prioritize innovation as the top priority but also back that up with actual investments. "Skeptical innovators" (30 percent) are companies that neither prioritize nor invest in innovation. Finally, "confused innovators" (25 percent) do not back up their stated priorities with investments in innovation. Of committed innovators, 60 percent generated increasing sales from recent launches (the past three years) compared with 30 percent and 47 percent by the skeptics and confused, respectively. What does this show?

For one thing, it shows that companies committed to innovation do a better job of recent launches. Now notice the variable of interest—sales

---

[1] www.bcg.com/en-us/publications/2021/most-innovative-companies-overview.

of new product launches. It seems as if even the "confused innovators" are putting out new product launches, but they are just being less successful. Why would that be the case? When a firm has formal procedures and incentives geared toward innovation, the new launches have been developed in the right framework with the right guidance and goal setting. The more haphazard approach to new launches would come from the confused innovators.

Thus, it's not just important to be doing new launches or even research. All efforts must be supported by an overall focus on innovation. When this complements research, the results can be remarkable.

It is important to have some formal frameworks, for example, a yearly formal or informal creative idea rejuvenation session. Further, to balance the short term with the long term, have a three- to five-year window to track trends and customer needs. It is also important to measure innovation productivity in financial terms.

One example is Target, which keeps pushing innovation by creating synergies between online and brick-and-mortar commerce. Target has innovated brilliantly through several initiatives, such as augmented-reality point-of-sale displays or omnichannel customer journeys, allowing customers to seamlessly shift from brick-and-mortar to online by, for instance, ordering at home and picking up in stores. In terms of innovation focus, what has driven all this innovation is that Target has made real investments and has doubled capital expenditure from 2016 to 2018. Target's online sales have grown far faster than its competition in 2019 and generated 25 percent annualized TSR in the years 2017, 2018, and 2019 in a market that has been under attack by players such as Amazon. And all this just a few years after the company was embroiled in a massive data breach scandal that could have seriously impacted its credibility and sales in the long term.[2]

---

[2] J.L. Yang, and A. Jayakumar. January 10, 2014. "Target Says up to 70 Million More Were Hit by December Data Breach," *The Washington Post.* www .washingtonpost.com/business/economy/target-says-70-million-customers-were-hit-by-dec-data-breach-more-than-first-reported/2014/01/10/0ada1026-79fe-11e3-8963-b4b654bcc9b2_story.html.

Companies should put their money where their mouth is and not just indulge in "innovation theater," which is any innovation initiative meant only to signal that innovation is happening, without any business impact.[3] There needs to be a focused emphasis on innovation, repeatedly and consistently. Sanjay had a client who was ostensibly interested and invested in innovation. However, these words were never backed up by action. Like David, there were always other practices that came with a higher priority. For many companies, innovation is a buzzword and what the cool companies do. However, when it comes to making tough decisions and prioritizing, they often don't end up sustaining an innovation focus. Going back to Sanjay's client, they are doing fine but, in his estimation, will never really be known as disruptive, nor will they be able to maintain their advantage. In their short-term quest for sales, they have ignored innovation's importance and will pay the price in the future.

In the conversation you heard earlier, you can easily imagine David saying, "all that is fine, but I have other more important priorities to attend to." While that may be true, myopia is no substitute for building an innovative culture attentive to forces on the horizon. A company that does not prioritize and, intentionally, deliberately emphasize innovation will not be consistently innovative. Much like the BCG list of companies that are one-hit wonders, they may be innovative one year but uncertain in the next.

Key Takeaways

- Have a formal, deliberate, and intentional approach toward fostering innovation. Have at least a quarterly meeting solely focused on company innovation. Ideally, innovation will be an agenda item in regularly scheduled meetings.
- Have at least a yearly formal or informal creative idea development process.

---

[3] A. Moazed. n.d. "What Is 'Innovation Theater'? A Definition, and How to Avoid It," *Applico*. www.applicoinc.com/blog/what-is-innovation-theater-a-definition-and-how-to-avoid-it/.

- Commitment toward innovation is key: prioritize innovation and back that up with committed investments toward innovation.
- Do not get caught up in other priorities ("there are far more important, immediate priorities"); no matter how urgent the other priorities may be, do not lose track of the intentional prioritizing of innovation as a means of growth.
- Set up formal incentives, rewards, and checkpoints for innovation; measure innovation productivity in financial terms.

CHAPTER 11

Don't Forget the Steps

Processes

"Did you have a to-do list, a template for innovation?" asked David, devotedly trying to pick the last few remnants of his slider from his plate.

"We had a very simple process that worked for us."

"How did they work? How did you measure success?"

"Laura did all that," said Peter.

"Who's Laura?" asked David incredulously.

"She's behind a lot of what you see in my company."

"What does she do?" asked David.

"She's a consultant. Top notch. She had all the processes mapped out. She also had the key success metrics. Slowly, over time, it started showing."

*   *   *

If you're going to make a great soup, you've got to have all the right tools in place: the pot, the ladle, the mixing bowls, the containers of spices, and so much more. Similarly, the tools or processes you bring to your organization, both informal and formal, help create the backdrop for innovation culture. A key question to ask right from the outset is: Does the organization have such processes in place? For example, is there a process to routinely test new ideas, products, or other developments? Does the organization have processes that allow for networking, for acquiring new skills? Is the organization able to quickly change some of its processes when they're no longer working? This section delineates many such processes, describing the importance of this dimension of innovation culture and pointing readers toward actions you can take now to put the right tools in place.

At first glance, it may seem that process and innovation clash with one another. Isn't one about formal structure while the other is about free-wheeling, creative developments? This divide collapses when highlighting "innovation-focused processes." You need a process for innovation, and you need to intentionally develop it. Much as a surfer needs a surfboard to ride the constantly changing motion of the waters below them, the right tools can make us more rather than less innovative. What is an innovation-focused process? In simple terms, it is the merging of discipline with creative ideation to develop specific steps that help move from ideation to production to completion.

At the same time, it's worth recognizing that process, structure, and methods can sometimes also be boxes that stifle innovation when they are maintained too rigidly. The trick is in finding the right balance. An innate part of this is the ability to pivot, change, and be nimble in processes. Furthermore, when it comes to innovation process design, one size or one method does not fit all. You need a range of tools at the ready. The way you create an innovation process for product design will be drastically different than the one you develop for your consumer-focused R&D methodologies. Innovation in how you approach R&D and consumer market research will have to differ from product design in both its execution and from a regulatory perspective. You may approach consumers for feedback on both, but the rules governing how, and the most effective methods for getting the feedback needed for each department will be unique.

Processes work synergistically with collaboration, empathy, personal creativity, freedom, and informal networking, many of the other dimensions of innovation readiness our research has unearthed. For instance, there is a useful and free website (at least until the time of writing) called "liberating structures" that provide 33+ processes for building inclusive and engaging meetings, for an innovative process that has collaboration, empathy, and informal networking built into its steps.[1] Most ways everyone tends to organize themselves at work

---

[1] See "Introduction," Liberating Structures. www.liberatingstructures.com.

(e.g., solo presentations to a passive group, open discussions lacking structure where the dominant voices and usual suspects always talk while others are excluded in patterned ways), tend to be the least inclusive and engaging processes possible. Liberating structures such as 1-2-4-All (where people have to spend some time individually working through a problem, then share out in pairs, then sift ideas in groups of four, before sharing out key revelations/themes with a whole group) provide an organization with a tool that heats and mixes the soup—providing a template for innovation readiness.

There are many more processes that can be put in play to build a culture of innovation. Every year, the number of research-backed tools for doing so has only been on the increase, both from the literature and from practical experiments. HubSpot provides a notable example.[2] The company follows a program called "refactoring," which involves changing how a program works internally without changing the output, to make it more efficient. For example, this could mean eliminating a longstanding report that nobody uses or simply getting rid of unproductive meetings that are relics of a bygone era.

Dyer, Gregersen, and Christenson describe several processes that successful, innovative companies follow, such as questioning, observing, internal and external networking, and experimentation. Toyota, using a process tool called the "five-whys," is a perfect example of using a supported process of questioning to lead employees toward innovation. Observation involves not only customers but other companies as well—such as Google observing P&G's launch and providing feedback that was significant for the company. In fact, the two conglomerates had also set up a process of information sharing in which the two swapped employees, with employees spending weeks dipping into each other's staff training programs and sitting in on meetings where business plans get hammered out.[3]

---

[2] R. Steffens. January 04, 2019. "How HubSpot Nailed Workplace Culture (And What You Can Learn From Them)," *Bluleadz*. www.bluleadz.com/blog/how-hubspot-nailed-workplace-culture-what-to-learn.

[3] E. Byron. November 19, 2008. "A New Odd Couple: Google, P&G Swap Workers to Spur Innovation," *The Wall Street Journal*. www.wsj.com/articles/SB122705787917439625.

Another great example of a process fueling innovation is the "innovator's challenge" hosted by Google four times a year. The challenge has employees pitch ideas to senior management that are awarded and rewarded. Another Google process is to have ideas posted on an internal electronic platform that employees can provide feedback on and rate. This allows the selection of winning ideas that can be produced, much like the early stage prototyping typical of design thinking. P&G's "connect and develop" is another process that is focused on getting half of its new ideas, technologies, and products from external sources.[4] For this, it partners with NineSigma, a technology company providing Managed Exchange, a platform that matches technology seekers with solutions. Similarly, Reckit Benkeiser offers IdeaLink, a platform that allows innovators from across the world to submit ideas to the company.[5] All these approaches underscore how, with the right tools at hand, innovation goes from a buzzword to a concrete reality driving measured results.

Peter Skarzynski and Rowan Gibson describe in detail how Whirlpool underwent an entire process to unleash innovation in their company.[6] In step one, 75 highly talented people from across the company's three geographic regions across the world were put in a team tasked with developing an innovation process that could be adopted company wide. Initially there were concerns that the company could not afford to pull important employees out of their operational roles, but they still made it happen as a mark of their commitment to this goal.

It is important to realize that, just as with David's company and most other organizations, there were other activities that Whirlpool could have spent its time and efforts on. It chose to invest its resources deliberately and intentionally in creating processes for innovation that would yield benefits down the road. This team developed key strategic insights and generated hundreds of ideas based on these ideas. The team designed ways

---

[4] "P&G in two-year deal with NineSigma," *Cincinnati Business Courier*, March 19, 2003, www.bizjournals.com/cincinnati/stories/2003/03/17/daily31.html.

[5] https://www.reckitt.com/innovation/submit-an-idea/.

[6] P. Skarzynski, and R.Gibson. 2008. *Innovation to the Core: A Blueprint for Transforming the Way Your Company Innovates* (Harvard Business Review Press).

to select and systematically identify the important ones, build business plans based on these ideas, and deliver a means of taking these business plans to market.

After this, a third of the 75 employees went back to their regions and operational units, a third became innovation consultants within the company, and a third stayed on to implement the innovation projects that emerged. The teams still exist and have yielded many successful ventures to the company. The process has become part of the culture and many more employees from across the company have participated in the groups. Furthermore, Whirlpool also set up innovation boards made from senior leaders from three regions.

The company had to spend at least half a day once a month to review its progress on innovation and ongoing innovation projects. This made innovation take center stage, instead of execution and day-to-day operations. The board even made innovation a top management priority. Board members had to foster innovation and were also made accountable for other employees to devote regular work hours to pursue innovation—apparently about 10 to 15 percent of regular hours were spent on innovation.

Processes must be set by a corporation to drive innovation and make it part of the organization's culture. Procter & Gamble, the world's leading consumer packaged goods company, seemed to have lost its steam in terms of disruptive innovation and was grappling with intense competition from smaller, more agile, direct-to-consumer companies, such as the Dollar Shave Club. Kathy Fish was asked to head Research, Development, and Innovation in 2014 and embarked on an ambitious Growth Operating System in 2016 (Truelove et al.) using what she called the "Growthworks" strategy.[7] She was convinced that every employee of P&G (about 100,000 strong) should recognize the importance of innovation not only in terms of product, but in all aspects of consumer experience. She launched Growthworks, which brought lean innovation to P&G. Inspired by the entrepreneurial "growth" mindset, this initiative

---

[7] For a detailed account of Growthworks, see E. Truelove, L.A. Hill, and E. Tedards. July 10, 2020. "Kathy Fish at Procter & Gamble: Navigating Industry Disruption by Disrupting from Within," *Harvard Business Review*.

was aimed at bringing the agility of startups to the efficiency-based, rigidly structured processes within P&G. This experience has taught them that it is also important to ensure that the big company does not interfere with the agility and entrepreneurial nature of the small company culture.

A quick Google search for "processes for innovation" will lead you to several pages of information. Each approach is different, with different steps. What's not important for innovation is that you necessarily stick with any one tool; it's better to search far and wide, selecting from the many processes available that can suit a deliberate, intentional approach toward innovation. For example, according to the *MIT Sloan Review*, there are five stages of successful innovation: idea generation and mobilization, advocacy and screening, experimentation, commercialization, and diffusion and implementation.[8] This model builds on research from more than 30 U.S. and European companies and their annual reports prescribing these stages.

Yet another model looks at three steps of the innovation process: insight, identifying problems, and producing a solution.[9] There are as many approaches, prescriptions, and steps as there are authors. The key here is that it's the presence of a process that creates a systematic approach toward innovation.

The specific process needs to be customized and specific to context, industry, and case. While the prescriptive, one-size-fits-all models are based on solid theory and work in certain industries, they are not a guarantee of success in all organizations. Each context has its own unique challenges and circumstances.

Overall, processes should be systematic, repeatable, and consistent. Innovation is not occasional or in response to a specific threat, but a sustained process that makes sure innovation is a continuous part of the culture. That's the key. A "process" can be as simple as Google setting up

---

[8] A. Mariello. April 01, 2007. "The Five Stages of Successful Innovation," *MIT Sloan Management Review*. https://sloanreview.mit.edu/article/the-five-stages-of-successful-innovation/.

[9] "The Innovation Process: 3 Steps to Improving Your Facility," *Precor*. www.precor.com/en-us/resources/the-innovation-process-3-steps-to-improving-your-facility.

the "20 percent project" (referred to earlier in Chapter 8) or using the open source "liberating structures" tools referred to earlier in this chapter. Go for simple, elegant, and effective.

Key Takeaways

- Processes come from merging disciplines with creative ideation to develop specific steps that help move from ideation to production to completion.
- Processes for innovation must be deliberate, elaborate, and intentional; however, they cannot be cookie cutter for all facets of the organization. They should be designed with the goals and circumstances of each department, functional unit, or group in mind.
- Processes must foster but not hinder or put hurdles in the way of innovation; balance is key.
- Be nimble and ever evolving with processes—use methods such as the five-whys, observing, internal and external networking, experimentation, or liberating structures to fine tune processes.
- Customize by creating specific processes depending on your industry and case. Overly prescriptive, one-size-fits-all models may not work; they at least need to be customized.

CHAPTER 12

Be Fluid

Flexibility

"So, you outsourced your innovation huh?" asked David sarcastically.

"You mean Laura?"

David nodded.

"Not really. She helped but it was us who made it happen," said Peter.

"I know, I am just kidding dude."

A bit like a sibling teasing the other, David was giving Peter a hard time. While he did want the information, he did not want Peter to know he did. He did not want to give that power to Peter.

"Let's talk about something else," said Peter.

"No, no! I want to talk about this."

"What else do you want to know?" asked Peter.

"Everything. How did the transformation happen? You make it sound so easy, I am sure it wasn't," said David.

"No, it wasn't!"

"What was your biggest challenge?"

"Well, one big one was striking the right balance. We needed templates and processes and yet at the same time needed to have flexibility."

*   *   *

Part of the art and science of truly great soup making is being able to pivot on the fly. In fact, you'll often hear cooks use words like "flexible" and "improvise" as critical components of what it takes to make soups taste better.[1] Similarly, a truly innovative organization needs to be flexible: without high degrees of centralization, formalization, and bureaucracy. A bureaucratic, rule-heavy organization will find it difficult to be innovative because most innovative efforts will be squelched by the institution's very structure. Flexibility can be either adaptive (i.e., in response to an external stressor or challenge) or spontaneous (i.e., being flexible without any challenges or distress).

Lipshitz and Waingortin provide an interesting example of adaptive flexibility: there was a hotel whose customers complained about the elevators being slow.[2] Replacing the elevators would be a huge expense. The hotel hired a psychologist who figured out that the problem was due to boredom, not the actual speed of the elevator. The psychologist suggested installing mirrors in front of the lifts to keep customers entertained while waiting for the elevators. Lo and behold, the complaints stopped. Another example of adaptive flexibility is "jugaad." Jugaad is a Hindi word roughly meaning "an innovative fix, an improvised solution" and is a unique way of thinking in response to a challenge.[3] The authors argue that Jugaad innovation is practiced not just in India but followed by entrepreneurs across the world (e.g., it's called *gambiarra* in Brazil, and *zizhu chuangxin* in China). Such forms of adaptive flexibility allow firms to get out of difficult situations, to see problems from a fresh perspective, and identify new ways of problem solving.

Imagine a hot new startup built on the radical ideas of its founder. The founder puts together a fantastic team, they hit it off, and, as a "band of pirates" (Steve Jobs famously said, "it's better to be a pirate than join the navy") they set about creating a huge splash.[4] An innovative product

---

[1] "A basic soup or stew is nourishing, inexpensive, and flexible," EatFresh. https://eatfresh.org/healthy-lifestyle/shopping-and-budgeting-cooking/basic-soup-or-stew-nourishing-inexpensive-and.

[2] R. Lipshitz, and M. Waingortin. 1995. "Getting Out of Ruts," *Journal of Creative Behavior* 23, pp. 151–171.

[3] N. Radjou, J. Prabhu, and S. Ahuja. 2012. *Jugaad Innovation: Think Frugal, Be Flexible, Generate Breakthrough Growth* (Jossey-Bass), p. 4.

[4] K. Leswing. April 01, 2016. "Apple Is Flying a Pirate Flag Over Its Headquarters—Here's Why," *Business Insider*. www.businessinsider.com/apple-is-flying-a-pirate-flag-over-its-headquarters-today-heres-why-2016-4.

takes off, it is disrupting the world, and we are all in a better place for it. Now what happens? This is where the devil is truly in the details. Success often tends to create inertia, both structural and cultural. The same band of radical pirates, with their own breakthrough vision of how the world could work, start to believe that their original way of doing things is the only way. If the environment changes, the very same innovative startup can easily fail to adapt and be flexible. This is the classic pattern that many entrepreneurial successes face: scaling up brings bureaucracy, a strict adherence to rules, red tape, and a lack of flexibility as the ground shifts beneath everyone's feet. This is also emblematic of the efficiency–flexibility tradeoff that has long been recognized. The idea is that efficiency implies a rigid adherence to structure, and rules fly in the face of flexibility. Can they both coexist? Is it an oxymoron to suggest that an organization be efficient and flexible at the same time?

There are some solutions to this seeming bind. One of the first practices is for companies to view the importance of both efficiency and flexibility and not see them in conflict. One way to do that is to consistently pursue entrepreneurial thinking and approaches. A famous example is P&G. As discussed earlier, the "Growthworks" approach was rooted in this philosophy. The idea was to mine the inherent flexibility in entrepreneurial firms and combine that with the inherent efficiency of a behemoth like P&G. There are, in fact, several organizations that have understood the importance of this approach, such as The Garage Group, a firm based in Cincinnati, OH, that claims to "bring lean innovation approaches to future-proof Big Cos."[5]

The other solution is to manage the two through the life cycle of the firm—understanding that while efficiency may be conducive to continuous innovation, flexibility is even more important for disruption. Efficiency is valuable during continuous innovation stages—with cost and lead time reductions that can be achieved through stage gate models and lean principles. However, when the external environment is changing or has changed, radical or breakthrough innovation becomes fundamental.

---

[5] "Home Page," The Garage Group. www.thegaragegroup.com/.

Such situations are replete with newness, uncertainty, and ambiguity that simply demand flexibility.

There's the famous case of Kodak, the innovator in film technology who unfortunately could not adapt to a changing environment. And, of course, Blockbuster video, a VHS rental company that remained static in the face of enormous industry changes, including the shift to digital streaming and the rise of Netflix. Think of David and his company during the Covid pandemic. In such situations, the systems set in place by his father hindered adaptation. If David, like Peter, had adopted a more flexible approach during the pandemic, during the time when such an approach was needed, then the company likely would have survived.

Another strategy is to build efficient systems but also be open to destruction, pivoting, and change in times of need. Read that again: a company needs to be open to *destroying* what it has created if changes in the environment warrant it.[6] This requires positioning one's mindset between structure and spontaneity. In Weick and Sutcliffe's formulation, this commitment to flexibility means that one must get comfortable with unpredictability and improvisation:

> Greater skill at improvisation is a way to increase one's commitment to resilience and to act on a greater variety of surprises. If a limited action repertoire limits perception, then increased skill at improvisation enlarges the potential actions available in one's repertoire, which should broaden the range of cues that you can afford to notice and handle. For example, medication errors were reduced 66 percent when a pharmacist was added to a team of doctors and nurses making rounds in an intensive care unit. By expanding its repertoire of capabilities, the medical team was able to notice more mistakes and correct them before they became catastrophes. . . . If [a company leader] is not at once *improvising* and improvising *warily*, he is not engaging his somewhat trained wits in a partly fresh situation. It is the pitting of an acquired

6 M.L. Tushman, and C.A. O'Reilly III. 1996. "Ambidextrous Organizations: Managing Evolutionary and Revolutionary Change," *California Management Review* 38, no. 4, pp. 8–30. doi:10.2307/41165852.

competence or skill against unprogrammed opportunity, obstacle, or hazard.[7]

So, what specifically does bureaucracy bring that would stifle such innovation? For one, formalization, which is the degree to which rules, procedures, instructions, and communications are formalized.[8] An over-reliance on such formalization cuts down on experimentation, on the freedom to make mistakes, and reduces the chances that employees may choose to deviate from sanctioned or ordained behavior.[9] In that sense, bureaucracies can curb exploratory behaviors, adaptive thinking, and innovation. David's company is a perfect example of formalization ruining innovation.

Formalization encourages clichéd, repetitive responses to stimuli.[10] In fact, that's the goal of formalization: it is aimed at reducing variance; it is aimed at standardizing and codifying. Companies codify best practices to make them more efficient and easier to implement.[11] Bureaucracy is another term for this sort of formalization and codification.

Such methods might work well in nondynamic, predictable, and repeatable environments, like stable manufacturing plants. But when traditionally stable companies experience turbulence along factors such as their supply chains, the need for flexibility is now demanded of everyone.

---

[7] K.E. Weick, and K.M. Sutcliffe. 2015. *Managing the Unexpected: Sustained Performance in a Complex World* (Hoboken: Wiley), p. 99, p. 69, emphasis in original.

[8] P.N. Khandwalla. 1977. *The Design of Organizations* (New York, NY: Harcourt Brace Jovanovich).

[9] K.E. Weick. 1998. "Introduction Essay—Improvisation as a Mindset for Organizational Analysis," *Organization Science* 9, no. 5, pp. 543–555. doi:10.1287/orsc.9.5.543.

[10] R.L. Daft, and R.H. Lengel. May 1986. "Organizational Information Requirements, Media Richness and Structural Design," *Management Science* 32, no. 5, pp. 554–571. doi:10.1287/mnsc.32.5.554.

[11] U. Zander, and B. Kogut. February 1995. "Knowledge and the Speed of the Transfer and Imitation of Organizational Capabilities: An Empirical Test," *Organization Science* 6, no. 1, pp. 76–92. doi:10.1287/orsc.6.1.76.

McDonalds tries to stay away from rigid structures and hierarchies. Vendors who supply ingredients, employees, and even customers are encouraged to develop innovative ideas. "Noodle teams" is the name the organization has come up with for its test kitchens where anyone can try their hand at new ideas and recipes.[12] In keeping with the test kitchen mentality, across the organization, hierarchies are flat, and anyone can reach out to anyone else.

Another perfect example of this is Patagonia: "We have a policy that when the surf comes up, you drop work and you go surfing," says Yvon Chouinard, in a recent interview on the NPR podcast, "How I Built This."[13] With this approach, the organization allows its employees to take a break and do something outdoors, even if it is during office hours. Similarly, employees of Atlassian get paid time off to devote to fun, charity, and their own personal development.[14]

Finally, the authors of the book *Humanocracy* discuss the importance of a lack of bureaucracy in innovation, asserting that "bureaucratic organizations are inertial, incremental and dispiriting."[15] In a telling and summative comment on the book, John Mackey, CEO of Whole Foods Market, wrote "Bureaucratic hierarchy is simply too slow in making decisions, and not innovative enough to be competitively successful in the third decade of the twenty-first century."[16] Those companies that position themselves as ready to pivot, come what may, will be the innovators of the next hundred years—so why not make your own organization the same?

---

[12] "Organizational Innovation Examples—Innovative Enterprises Fight Bureaucracy and Rigid Processes," *Innolytics*, n.d. https://innolytics-innovation.com/organizational-innovation-examples/.

[13] C. Clifford. December 23, 2016. "The Founder of Patagonia Fishes Half the Year and Tells His Employees to Go Surfing," *CNBC* . www.cnbc.com/2016/12/23/founder-of-patagonia-fishes-half-the-year-tells-his-employees-to-surf.html.

[14] "Best examples of company cultures that engage employees," Impraise. www.impraise.com/blog/best-examples-of-company-cultures-that-engage-employees.

[15] G. Hamel, and M. Zanini. 2020. "Humanocracy: Creating Organizations as Amazing as the People Inside them," Harvard Business Review Press.

[16] Hamel, and Zanini. "Humanocracy."

Key Takeaways

- A bureaucratic, rule-heavy organization will find it hard to be innovative; formalization encourages clichéd, repetitive responses to stimuli.
- Adaptive flexibility is key, as it helps organizations get out of difficult situations.
- Organizations need to see the importance of both flexibility and efficiency. Efficiency may be conducive to continuous innovation; flexibility is vital for disruptions.
- Build efficient systems but also be open to pivoting and change if needed.

CHAPTER 13

The Gravy

Resources

"Man, those sliders were delicious!" said David with a satisfied smile. "Best thing I did all day."

"I need another drink now. Can I get you something?" asked Peter nervously. He didn't really want David to get drunk.

"No man. I have had enough already—more than my usual."

"Be right back," said Peter. He came back a few minutes later with his drink, thankful that David was staying within his limits.

"What'd you get?"

"It's their mango IPA," said Peter. "By the way, did you give them a golden handshake? The people you fired?"

"Of course!" said David, pulling out a piece of debris from his teeth. "Pretty generous."

"Good!"

"It's tough times Peter. We are hurting, pockets are not as deep anymore."

"I know. Did you ever have anything earmarked for innovation?"

"What do you mean?"

"Did you ever have any sort of resources set aside purely for innovative activity?"

"You mean like R&D?"

"Not just R&D. A general set of resources—people, time, and especially capital."

"Nah, not really. My dad believed if we kept costs low and delivered value to the customer, the rest was unimportant."

"What do you think?"

"I bought into that originally. Now I see the folly."

"It might have been worth the investment?"

"I think so. Putting our money where the mouth is so we could have been forward-looking and ready to pivot, not just trying to sustain the way things had always been."

*   *   *

Does your organization have resources and rewards—monetary and nonmonetary—set aside for innovation? Resources are required for a truly innovative culture to flourish. An organization that does not set aside and direct resources, both human and capital, toward innovation will have a tough time responding to new developments and forging ahead successfully in the future. One fundamental fact can't be lost here: no soup is made without a cook going out and buying the ingredients to make the product. If you didn't put any money or time into getting all that's needed in the first place to make the soup happen, you'd be left with a watery mess.

Phil McKinney, a renowned innovation expert, talks about the "Law of Resources" as one of the immutable principles of innovation.[1] "Innovation requires a committed level of resources (people, money, time, equipment) over an extended period of time," he argues. McKinney says that companies break this law by half-baked commitments to innovation, benchmarking and comparing only the investment side, cutting back resource commitments in times of financial challenge, and making only quarterly or annual commitments, which limit the work innovation teams put in so they can deliver on time. The key is a continued, consistent pledge, not temporary or reactive commitments.

Resources can be either tangible (e.g., financial, office or other spaces, tech or other equipment needed) or intangible (e.g., knowledge, professional development, group capabilities)—both are important for innovation. Resources need to be directed specifically toward innovation. That

---

[1] P. McKinney. n.d. "The 7 Immutable Laws of Innovation—Follow Them or Risk the Consequences," Phil McKinney. https://philmckinney.com/the-7-immutable-laws-of-innovation-follow-them-or-risk-the-consequences/.

means hiring for innovation, rewarding for innovation, and creating circumstances and situations that promote innovation as part of planning. In fact, Epstein and colleagues investigated the importance of eight characteristics of leaders in enabling creativity by surveying 1,337 managers from 19 countries.[2] They found that "provides adequate and appropriate competency" proved to be the most valuable managerial competency in enabling creativity.

Tangible financial resources are critical for equipment, employee hiring and budgeting, tools for innovative exploration, and more. They can also be used as rewards. We earlier spoke about the importance of intrinsic motivation, that the tasks and goals themselves be inherently rewarding, without any financial incentives. Yet extrinsic motivation in the form of rewards can play a key role in providing fuel for innovation. Some evidence exists against the use of too much extrinsic motivation, such as financial remuneration or even recognition. With an overreliance on trying to both meet expectations and appease or satisfy the external resources, people can too easily lose sight of the internal joy and drives that can push just about anyone through a demanding set of tasks.

P&G uses funds directed toward new business that are sometimes kept separate from the profit and loss statement, especially at the initial stages of breakthrough platform testing. Crest Whitestrips was able to be developed by an innovation fund that was not limited by the considerations of the company's current profit and loss. This gave the organization sufficient flexibility to inject resources into the development of the product.[3]

However, extrinsic motivation can make people stick to tasks and their implementation. Consistently, Caniels and colleagues found that

---

[2] R. Epstein, K. Kaminaka, V. Phan, and R. Uda. 2013. "How Is Creativity Best Managed? Some Empirical and Theoretical Guidelines," *Creativity and Innovation Management* 24, no. 4, pp. 359–374. doi:10.1111/caim.12042.

[3] In an interview with S. Mitra, former senior vice president of Global Innovation and a member of P&G's top leadership team, the Global Leadership Council. Post retirement from P&G, he has spent seven years as a board member and strategic advisor to several F500 companies and new ventures. www.linkedin.com/in/shekhar-mitra-ph-d-4b427b47/.

extrinsic motivation works better in certain parts of the creative process, with extrinsic motivation being more important in the later implementation stages.[4] They found that idea generation can be inhibited by external motivators. Creative people prefer to keep agnostic about audiences or any other audience that they may have to face in the initial phases of their work. They indulge in the creative idea generation process mostly for the sheer pleasure of doing so. Solving the problem can be its own reward for a time, so it's critical to separate divergent from convergent phases for innovation.[5]

Even idea promotion was found to be driven by intrinsic motivation, a deep-felt belief in the idea itself. Yet the importance of financial resources comes in the form of human resource time directed toward setting up the process (which involves labor for the books) and required infrastructure for all aspects of innovation leading to implementation. No matter how creative an idea, it's of no use if it doesn't see the light of day. So, resources aren't just a nice add-on to innovation; they are central to its very presence in an organization.

According to Mark McGuiness, financial reward is a way of keeping score, of knowing how much your employer values your contribution, just as an artist measures her success by how much money her audience is paying.[6] Awards, similarly, are a measure of success, appreciation, and value.

Although used interchangeably, R&D and innovation are not the same. R&D is a component of innovation that also includes the commercialization or capitalization of knowledge. R&D tends to be technical and internally focused, whereas innovation is broader and includes external stakeholders and scanning. R&D should be an investment in innovation.

---

[4] M.C.J. Caniels, K. De Stobbeleir, I. De Clippeleer. June 2014. "The Antecedents of Creativity Revisited: A Process Perspective," *Creativity and Innovation Management* 23, no. 2, pp. 96–110. doi:10.1111/caim.12051.

[5] K. Boogaard. September 04, 2018. "Convergent Thinking vs. Divergent Thinking: Why Planning Isn't Always the Right Thing to Do," *Wrike*. www.wrike.com/blog/convergent-thinking-vs-divergent-thinking/.

[6] M. McGuinness. February 03, 2022. "Lesson 21: What Motivation Does to Your Creativity," *The 21st Century Creative*. https://lateralaction.com/motivation-creativity/.

Its importance can also vary from industry to industry. Studying 100-plus Chinese automobile companies led Wang and Banister to conclude that financial resources, R&D, human capital, innovation leadership, and collaborative culture are key drivers of innovation.[7]

Overall, leaders and managers must invest in innovation on many different levels. Tangible and intangible resources that can fuel innovation constitute an important part of building innovation culture. And to this mix, the resources that can be brought or provided to diverse people can create even more robust places and spaces for innovation to flourish.

Key Takeaways

- Resources, both human and capital, are required for a truly innovative culture to flourish.
- Organizations should be committed to a continued, consistent pledge of resource investment, not temporary or reactive commitments.
- Resources are both tangible (such as financial, tech, and equipment) and intangible (such as knowledge and professional development). Build line items for these resources in your budgets.
- Resources are needed to create both intrinsic and extrinsic motivation for employees.

---

[7] L. Wang, J.L. Jin, and D. Banister. January 27, 2019. "Resources, State Ownership and Innovation Capability: Evidence From Chinese Automakers," *Creativity and Innovation Management* 28, no. 2, pp. 203–217. https://doi.org/10.1111/caim.12305.

CHAPTER 14

Add Variety

Diversity

"How's your Mango IPA?" asked David.

"Really good! Hoppy, with subtle notes of mango," said Peter.

"Notes of mango? Sounds like a girl's drink!" mocked David with a smile.

"That's very sexist," said Peter.

David was about to contest the assertion but checked himself. "Sorry, I guess you're right," he admitted.

"Blame it on Dad?" asked Peter mischievously.

"Well, my company *is* a bunch of white guys dude," complained David.

"But seriously, does it really matter to you that all your employees are white males?" asked Peter.

"Quite frankly, it doesn't. I just keep getting told that it shouldn't be. I don't get it."

"That's hilarious," said Peter, chuckling. "He's got a *lot* of learning to do here," he thought to himself, still chuckling.

*   *   *

Diversity is critical for innovation, but why? What specifically is it about having people from different backgrounds, with different identities, and with unique needs and interests that drives innovation? How do race, gender, and other variables predict innovativeness?

Diversity is important not only in terms of the obvious manifestations, such as age, gender, and race. What drives innovation is also diversity in perspective, experience, education, and training, among other variables, and having different people in your organization increases the likelihood of reaping all of diversity's benefits for both the company and its people. There are many works that explain how historical and contemporary structures and inequities demand diverse, equitable, and inclusive workplaces. Given space considerations and our immediate interest in how diversity sparks innovation, we refer readers to the depth and breadth of the sources found in this footnote.[1]

For our present purposes, diversity can be defined as "innate diversity" (age/gender/race, etc.) and "acquired diversity" (education/experiences/viewpoints, etc.). In a large survey conducted by Forbes, of 321 companies with revenues greater than $500 million, a whopping 85 percent agreed or strongly agreed that diversity is key to innovation.[2] The report states: "Competition for talent is fierce in today's global economy, so companies need to have plans in place to recruit, develop, and retain a diverse workforce." Survey respondents reported that some areas of diversity, such as age and disability, have been harder to improve, begging greater efforts to create equitable conditions for all.

---

[1] Some works to start with include F. Dobbin, and A. Kalev. July–August 2016. "Why Diversity Programs Fail," *Harvard Business Review*. https://hbr .org/2016/07/why-diversity-programs-fail; G. Morse. July–August 2016. "How to Design Bias Free Organizations," *Harvard Business Review*. https:// hbr.org/2016/07/designing-a-bias-free-organization; J. Gilhool. June 03, 2013. "Going Global? Better Rethink Your Diversity Training," *Forbes*. https://bit .ly/2znePW5; Larger works on structural racism across society include I. Kendi. 2019. *How to be an Antiracist* (New York, NY: One World); I. Oluo. 2018. *So You Want to Talk About Race* (New York, NY: Seal Press); R. Rothstein. 2017. *The Color of Law* (New York, NY: Liveright Publishing). A great diversity, equity, and inclusion reading list can be found at: https://libguides.library.umkc.edu/ ld.php?content_id=62834289.

[2] D. Tencer. July 29, 2011. "Forbes Survey: Workplace Diversity Key To Innovation," *HuffPost Canada*. www.huffingtonpost.ca/2011/07/29/workplace-diversity-innovation_n_913214.html.

A similar ranking is reported by Stuart Levine, writing in Forbes.[3] Levine's report looked at diversity among companies belonging to the S&P 500 and found that "Diverse and inclusive cultures are providing companies with a competitive edge over their peers." There is a substantial and growing body of evidence showing that diverse groups are more innovative and productive.

One of the pitfalls of talking about diversity is that it can too quickly lack substance or bypass needed changes, becoming simply symbolic or a publicity tool for organizations. What organizations need to realize is that attending to diversity is a market imperative. In a scathing attack on what he calls the "fraud of diversity," William Powell rails against the lack of true cultural pluralism hiding behind a mad rush by organizations to tick the appropriate boxes to create an "HR metric and a really cool definition that's supposed to make us feel warm, gooey and accepting."[4] He argues that everyone now generally agrees on the harmful consequences of lacking diversity, but "without embracing the reason behind the need for diversity, the how and the why of it all go painfully unnoticed." This simply cannot continue, as the United States and other countries are "at an inflection point regarding gender, race, and similar variables, and without full inclusion society will fail to maximize its talents and organizations of all types will lose legitimacy," connecting "firmly with calls from vast, cross-disciplinary literatures—warranting both attention and change."[5]

First, a diverse workforce represents the diverse marketplace for every organization. It's a simple equation: the better represented the marketplace within the organization, the better its market orientation. The better the organization understands its consumers, the better it can innovate for its market. Diverse teams are better able to understand unmet market

[3] S.R. Levine, and Thought Leaders. January 15, 2020. "Diversity Confirmed To Boost Innovation And Financial Results," *Forbes.* www.forbes.com/sites/forbesinsights/2020/01/15/diversity-confirmed-to-boost-innovation-and-financial-results/?sh=54b73461c4a6.

[4] W. Powell. July 28, 2011. "Why Workplace Diversity Is a Fraud," *Business 2 Community.* www.business2community.com/leadership/why-workplace-diversity-is-a-fraud-046703.

[5] D. Waisanen. 2021. *Leadership Standpoints: A Practical Framework for the Next Generation of Nonprofit Leaders* (Cambridge University Press), p. 12.

needs. If someone within a team is in any way like the consumer without, they are more likely to understand that consumer better. Levine reports that when there is at least one member in a group that shares the client's ethnicity, that team is twice as likely to understand that client's needs. The same holds for bigger markets and the consumer at large.

Second, diversity is important in the creative process. There are several reasons why diversity creates cognitive complexity. Steve Jobs is known to have often used William Plomer's words to define creativity as "connecting the unconnected."[6] The more diverse the group of people and their experiences, the richer the discussion, and the more they will reach far and wide for concepts and lenses that can be connected during the creative process. It's what Arthur Koestler has called "bisociation," which underscores that almost all creativity is generated by smashing together two unrelated planes of existence (or frames of reference) and seeing what sits at the intersections of those worlds.[7] Such creative moves simply cannot come into being without multicultural, multiform, and multiple identities in the mix of an organization's work.

In terms of process, diversity "jolts us into cognitive action in ways that homogeneity simply does not," says Columbia Business School professor, Katherine Phillips, describing her own and others' research for Scientific American in "How Diversity Makes Us Smarter."[8] She says that the heart of it is "informational diversity"—people coming from different backgrounds that bring a rich assortment of knowledge, thought, experiences, and perspectives to any situation. This array of people and perspectives forces the consideration of broader groups, opening the possibilities of collaborating with a wider set of solutions. Diverse group members set a foundation for unique and creative results.

In a study Phillips conducted, diverse groups outperformed homogenous ones in problem-solving tasks. In her words, "being with similar others leads us to think we all hold the same information and share the

---

[6] "William Plomer > Quotes," *Goodreads* www.goodreads.com/author/quotes/59133.William_Plomer.

[7] A. Koestler. 1964. *The Act of Creation* (New York, NY: Penguin Books).

[8] K.W. Phillips. October 2014. "How Diversity Makes Us Smarter," *Scientific American*. www.scientificamerican.com/article/how-diversity-makes-us-smarter/.

same perspective." The more homogenous a group, the more homogenous the thinking. "A big part of what I believe is that, fundamentally, we each have something truly unique to bring to the table," Simo Fidji, CEO, Instacart, told *Fortune* magazine.[9] "It's that diversity that's going to make it really fun for all of us to work together—and much more interesting and creative than if we were all made out of the same mold."

Sanjay has found the same results in leading groups through innovation labs and problem-solving workshops. Several other experiments and even large sets of data across multiple organizations have found conforming evidence that diversity enhances innovation. For example, Cristian Deszö of the University of Maryland and David Ross of Columbia University, who studied the composition of the top management of 1,500 firms of the S&P from 1992 through 2006, found that, on average, female representation in top management led to "an increase of $42 million in firm value,"[10] and that this improvement in firm performance was especially seen in firms that strategically emphasized innovation.

We could go on about the importance of diversity to innovation (and we urge readers to start exploring the many works linked to in our footnotes, as well as all that can be found in books, articles, and through professional development opportunities with your staff), but the important point is that this ingredient requires that you make every effort possible to have diverse people with different identities, backgrounds, cultural and subcultural perspectives, levels of training and field experiences, and more to your organization. Diversity isn't a nice add-on to an organization's work. It's now utterly clear that it's central to the very innovation that's even possible. If you're serious about building a culture of innovation and creating an organization aligned with 21st century demands, you'll need to make a new or renewed commitment to diversity as one of the key forces that can drive your products or services forward.

---

[9] M. Aspan. November 10, 2021. "Strategy Session: Instacart CEO Fidji Simo on How She Found Her Own Leadership Groove," *Fortune.* https://fortune.com/2021/11/10/instacart-ceo-fidji-simo-leadership-style/.

[10] C.L. Dezsö, and D.G. Ross. January 13, 2012. "Does Female Representation in Top Management Improve Firm Performance? A Panel Data Investigation," *Strategic Management Journal* 33, no. 9, p. 1080.

Key Takeaways

- Diversity in experience, perspective, thinking, identities, culture, and beliefs is vital for innovation.
- A diverse workforce represents the marketplace and different public, which helps the organization understand its market better.
- Informational diversity forces the group to consider the assortment of knowledge, thought, experiences, and perspectives needed to truly understand user needs and interests.
- Diversity promotes innovation, increasing cognitive flexibility and allowing groups to consider novel perspectives and thoughts that enhance the creative process.
- Groups with diverse members need to work harder and put themselves outside their comfort zones and tap into the knowledge and voices that exist in the room.

PART 3

Making the Soup

CHAPTER 15

Getting Help

"You've got to meet Laura!" said Peter.

"Do you honestly think my managers—Jim, Dave, Harmon, three 50+ year old white dudes—will listen to Laura?"

"Maybe if they don't, that's part of the problem."

"I guess you have a point," said David, grudgingly. "It's not me, it's getting everyone else to be on board, that's going to be the challenge."

"I think you will really benefit from Laura's work."

"What is so hotshot about what she does?"

"Well, first, she is all about measurement and assessment. She used a tool that assessed my innovation culture. It's called the InnoQ™. She makes the employees complete it; takes them about three to five minutes. It gives her a look under the hood, at the company culture and what's wrong with it."

"I have seen a lot of these diagnostics," said David, dismissively.

"This one is different dude. It has been tested and validated. It's short and simple, and yet gives a lot of information on the company. You know, the sort of things we talked about—collaboration and so on. The building blocks of an innovative culture."

"So, what then?"

"She identifies your company's weak spots and then makes concrete action plans to help improve the innovation culture. It's pretty detailed: she breaks it down and provides processes, templates, and specific actions for building and improving our innovation culture. It works man. At first, I was a skeptic but then realized it works."

"How can one person just show up and change the culture at my organization? We are talking about people who have been doing things a certain way for decades. Have you even met my team?" said David with some frustration and anger.

Peter looked at him. He knew this was coming; through the evening he was afraid there would be some confrontation. Fortunately, David did not drink as much as he feared, but there was a lot of pent-up frustration and bitterness. He needed to handle this very delicately. He just looked at David, and then, with a smile, simply said, "It worked for me David."

There was a long silence. David was about to launch into a retort but checked himself. He tried to take another sip of his now empty glass. He put it back on the table.

"I am trying to help, David."

"I know you are, but you sound like a professor in an MBA class, like an author of a self-help book. Reality is different man. Remember how we used to laugh at those books offering to transform our companies?"

"Just like everything else in life David, they are not all the same. Some are based on substance and work, some don't," said Peter.

David looked at him earnestly. He knew and trusted his friend.

"Even if I did bring her on board, how do you think she will do with my people? I know them man. They don't like change."

"David, I am sorry. You may not like what I am going to say," said Peter.

"Go on," said David, a little nervously.

"There comes a time when you have to take a stand. When it's not enough just to drown your sorrows in craft beer and blame your dad. I am sorry, if you really mean it and want to change, you must make it happen. It takes courage and conviction. You are the only one who can make it happen."

David remembered being in class with Peter. They would often disagree on assignments, but he had developed a high degree of respect for him. He also trusted Peter completely and knew that Peter had nothing to gain from helping him.

"Let me think about it," he said finally.

"Sure! It's your company, David," said Peter. "I am only trying to help because you asked or at least seemed to."

"Thanks man."

"Think about it," said Peter, punching something into his phone. "Here, I just texted you her details. Reach out to her if you feel like it. No harm done if not. She's very busy and I am not getting any kickbacks."

"OK."

"It's getting late," said Peter.

"Yeah, gotta get home."

"I've gotta run too, man. Nice seeing ya!"

"Same here buddy. Let's do this again."

"Absolutely!"

The meeting ended. It did leave an impression on David. He thought about the discussion a lot and finally came to a decision the next morning.

He took the number Peter gave him and gave Laura a call. After a few attempts at reaching back and forth, they finally connected.

CHAPTER 16

Getting the Ingredients Together

"Hi, Laura!"

"Hi David! How are you?" asked Laura.

"Doing well. Yourself?"

"Doing well, thanks!" said Laura.

"I've heard a lot about you, Laura."

"Thanks! Hopefully all good?" said Laura with a smile.

"Yes. You come highly recommended."

"I have read everything you shared with me. I am excited to help. However, let me warn you, it's not going to be easy or fast. What we're going to do needs sensitivity, empathy, and most of all, commitment."

"Are you going to be firing people?"

"No! But I would be asking to hire some new people to replace the ones you've let go. People from diverse backgrounds."

"What else?"

"Here." She pulled out a presentation.

"What is this?"

"It's the results of the InnoQ."

"What does it say?"

"Well, it shows that your biggest problem is your ranks and files do not share what your senior management thinks. You're living in two separate universes. An innovation culture is impossible with this kind of disconnect."

"So, we should fire them then?"

"Absolutely not. You've already done a lot of that. But I think you must face up to it, David. I am not going to sugar coat it. Would you rather call more people into your office and fire them or would you rather be honest and tell them there's a need for change? I personally think this is a good time. With your letting others go already, everyone has woken up and smelt the coffee. You need to use this opportunity to make your point—for radical change."

"OK, then what's that?"

"I have specific steps and courses of action for each of the 11 dimensions we've measured for the company. And you'll get to see how you're doing compared to your competition and within your industry. It sounds like you already got a taste of that through your conversation with your friend that you shared with me."

"Yes, that's true. But will this solve the problem?"

"It will start the process of change."

*   *   *

We will take a break from this story here. If you can't wait to find out what happened to David and his company, you can jump ahead to the Epilogue. However, at this point, we will take a turn to examine the Inno-Q™ and its genesis, so that readers can gain insight into how aspects of innovation can be tapped into and built out across an organization. You'll see a road test for the InnoQ™ in action. We'll then move to an overarching mindset and philosophy for practicing innovation culture, applied improvisation, and connections between the dimensions of innovation culture and larger developments with leadership, organizations, and societies. Finally, we'll provide you with a sequence of exercises that you can run with your teams to start building innovative activities into your work, from the ground up. Readers will learn how to use and implement improvisational and creative activities focused on developing innovative products, services, and for other outcomes.

PART 4

The Measurements— InnoQ™

CHAPTER 17

Genesis

So, are you following Peter and David through their journey at the brewery? Does it sound relatable? That was the idea—to make a point using simple, relatable examples. You've now read about all the ingredients that make up innovation soup. In Part 2 of this book, we now turn to a unique tool—leading to ways that you can use it to forward innovation in your organization. We are going to leave Peter and David alone for a little bit and pick their story up again in Part 4.

Based on the research Sanjay has conducted over the years on innovation culture, he decided to use his technical training to try to measure it. With his academic researcher hat on, there is one area in which he has done a lot of work: *measurement*. In fact, Sanjay is a self-described "measurement nerd." He has a spreadsheet that tracks everything he eats, drinks, thinks, and does, and every exercise he has done every day of his life for the past 20 years. The second author Don, who can't remember the last time he bothered using a tablespoon or a ruler, could not believe this when he first heard about it, thinking that Sanjay's superpower was being able to turn everything into big data. And it's true. At dinner, all of Sanjay's serving spoons are measuring cups and there are a plethora of kitchen scales spread across his kitchen and dining area—everything that goes in his body is measured. After all, there's the saying that "if you can't measure it, you can't improve it."[1]

Sanjay came up with a neat, four-item measurement devise that measures innovation culture, the InnoQ™. The best part is that it's not based solely on a CEO's opinion; it is grounded in the perspective of every employee, reaching all within an organization. Once the data are

---

[1] Attributed to P. Drucker, and S. Maital. "If You Can't Measure It, You Can't Improve It," *Waycare*, https://waycaretech.com/if-you-cant-measure-it-you-cant-improve-it/.

gathered, you can analyze, slice, and dice them any way you want. For instance, do you want to know if the sales department has a more innovative culture than accounting? Just ask the InnoQ™. Sanjay had a client a few years ago whose scores were off the charts, but there was a distinct difference in the scores along seniority—the senior management felt the culture was way more innovative than the middle- and junior-level managers: the classic ivory tower effect. The InnoQ™ is useful for seeing where alignment for innovation exists, while tapping into exactly when it is lacking in organizations.

There is a process for measurement in the social sciences. It is one thing to measure an ounce of chicken in the kitchen, but quite another to measure something like innovation culture. First, Sanjay performed focus groups and interviews to get a sense of what people thought "innovation readiness" means. Then he performed an extensive review of academic and practitioner literature. Synthesizing across the two steps, a set of survey questions started emerging (starting with 100+). Sanjay collected data using these survey questions. Based on the first round of data and statistical analysis, he deleted some items and changed some others.[2]

Then, Sanjay tested this model on fresh data and whittled it down further, changed more items, and so on, over and over again. When he finally arrived at a set of items and a structure that made sense (where cutting down any more items would only lead to data loss), he did what is called a "confirmatory factor analysis." He collected more data using this final set of items and completed additional statistical analysis to show that indeed the final set of items and structure worked. Rinse and repeat. The goal was to come up with a tool or survey that is comprehensive (like a 100-point inspection of your car at a dealership), doesn't miss anything, and, yet is not overly long because that would lead to respondent fatigue and a potentially poor quality of data.

What's detailed above is a simplified lay account of how measurement scales are developed. But we wanted readers to gain some background into all this to see the toil and sweat that went into trying to pinpoint with precision how innovation can be measured. The InnoQ™ is detailed

---

[2] For example, if there is very high correlation with other items, it means the item is superfluous or, if removing that item improves the model fit.

and yet the average time of completion for respondents has been about five minutes. But does it really work? Do the 11 dimensions really predict innovation? Does InnoQ™ itself accurately measure the 11 dimensions? For a final test, Sanjay took the InnoQ™ "on the road," inviting people to tell him about their company culture and innovation using the tool. Each organization received overall innovation readiness scores, and scores on each dimension benchmarked with national and industry averages. The following sections provide some further details about the tool's virtues in building and sustaining a highly innovative organization.

Bear in mind that the road test came far after the data collection needed for developing the survey took place. Also, at the time of the road test, Sanjay had only discovered 10 of the 11 dimensions. Consequently, the last dimension discussed in Part 2, *diversity*, was not included in this road test. Over 400 employees of various industries (15+ industries) across several companies completed this survey. Along with the 10 dimensions, survey participants were also asked how much they believed the company was innovative. It wasn't just one simple question, but a battery of six questions or items that capture features like how many patents an organization has and how many new products or lines have been produced (read more about this road test in the next chapter).

The neat thing about the InnoQ™ is that it lets you benchmark yourself against competition and the overall industry. Because all data come from real companies, you can find out not only how your company is doing, but also how your InnoQ™ compares to the national and industry averages.

So, not only can you compare the culture of R&D versus marketing, but you can also compare perceptions about this across industries and your competition. If your company leaders or other employees suspect innovation readiness (or the lack of it) has been the bottleneck to growth, not only are there now data, but also a clear roadmap of which specific dimension of readiness to focus on to improve overall innovativeness.

In terms of accuracy, InnoQ™ can recognize when an employee has "dialed it in." It knows whether respondents are doing a thoughtful job of responding to its questions. There is a simple algorithm for that having to do with the variance in the answers selected. Although this is proprietary software, only the thoughtful, deliberate responses are picked.

InnoQ™ is truly representative: it doesn't merely collect data from the top management, CEO, or HR functions. It collects data from every employee, across departments, levels of seniority, and branches/strategic business units (SBUs). What clients will get is an aggregated, comprehensive look at how ready *all* the employees think the organization is for innovation. Furthermore, the data can be sliced and diced by department, level, or branch/SBU, or any other means a client desires to perform more detailed comparisons.

Beyond the Obvious

Once the 11 dimensions are underscored with examples, it seems, well, kind of obvious right? Couldn't anyone have come up with the InnoQ™? Well, to this point, we'd note that nothing quite like it has been assembled formally using wide literatures and using empirical research—geared toward practices that can start tomorrow, day one at your work. "Why are you sharing proprietary information so publicly?" you might ask. Well, where knowledge is concerned, the more you give, the more you get. We are counting on your feedback, criticism, questions, and suggestions to add value to this research. Innovation doesn't occur in a vacuum; it's open to continued dialogue with diverse people. We see the recipe and ingredients for innovation soup as a starting point for building an outstanding, innovative organization, but it's not the end. As we push this work into the future, we need collaborative, cocreative individuals and teams to continue building upon this work. The real value of the InnoQ™ is in the data that have been collected. The research and wealth of literature collected over the years can't be replicated, but anyone who has completed or even just seen the InnoQ™ can copy and use its questions to continue forwarding this work in as many different iterations as can be imagined.

CHAPTER 18

The Road Test

Once perfected, InnoQ™ was put to the test on 100+ companies from 15+ industries. As seen in Table 18.1, companies in the top quartile of the InnoQ™ (i.e., the companies with the highest scores on innovation readiness) were 87 percent more innovative than those in the bottom quartile. That is strong support for InnoQ™ (for more details on the statistics, please refer to Appendix).

Table 18.1 Innovation and InnoQ™ score

InnoQ™ Score	Actual Innovation (Max = 30)	%	Actual Innovation Regressed on InnoQ™ Score
Bottom quartile	14.23	100	Regression coefficient (β) = 0.83, $p = 0.0001$*
Top quartile	26.7	187.6	

*: Highly significant

Key Insights:

Bureaucracy is rampant
Flexibility seems to be many industry's Achilles heel (see Tables A.2 and A.3)! Another way to look at flexibility would be as the opposite of bureaucracy. Employees of almost all industries (even the most innovative) seem to find a high degree of bureaucracy in their organizations. Scores on the flexibility dimension are generally very low across the board. Even the highest scoring industry on this dimension (Food & Beverages) only managed a score of 14.

Design thinking needed!
Empathy is critical for any company or industry both internally and externally. How can, for example, an apparel company design clothing that resonates with the consumer until they have an empathetic

understanding of the consumer? This also highlights the importance of adopting a design thinking approach in organizations.

Creativity killers

While people working in IT, marketing, and education seem to think of themselves as being creative more than other industries (not surprising), healthcare, hospitality, and consumer packaged goods (CPG) seem to lack personal creativity at the individual level. Is this a consequence of self-selection? In other words, do the "non-creatives" find themselves gravitating toward these industries? We think not. All human beings score at a genius level in creativity as children, yet our socialization and education processes kill this creativity. If you apply the same logic, it seems that some industries suck out the creativity of their employees! In contrast, some industries (Table A.2) seem to let their employees flourish creatively, which leads to higher levels of innovation.

Don't judge a book by its cover

It is surprising to see consumer packaged goods so far down the list on innovativeness (Table A.1). The industry is consumer-facing and advertising heavy (Est. $11.12 billion in digital advertising alone in 2019), bombarding us consumers with all forms of creative communication. Yet from inside it seems the farthest from being innovative! Advertising is usually created by third party ad agencies, so innovative advertising need not reflect a company's (or industry's) innovation.

So, that was a look at how the dimensions did on the road test. There is strong evidence that the ingredients are critically important for innovation soup and a strong innovation culture. As seen above, organizations with strong scores on the dimensions and, consequently, a strong innovation culture are also likely to be more innovative.

In the next part of this book, we build on these foundations. In this part, we tackle the importance of carrying on and keeping the "pot boiling." As we mentioned at this book's outset, besides the ingredients, this also requires an ability to "taste and adjust," that is, an ability to improvise well!

PART 5

Keeping the Pot Boiling

CHAPTER 19

Cooking With Gas

The Role of Improvisation

Let's talk about cooking with gas. Having lived in several different houses, Don has always noted the difference in feel and effect between electric and gas stoves. There's more than meets the eye here. To a skilled cook, it's the *responsiveness* of the gas, of turning a pan in different directions, of applying some heat and then backing off, that can turn a plain meat or vegetable dish into an extraordinary, flavorful creation greater than the sum of its parts. Where an electric range tends to cook food in a linear, uniform way—just plop on the object, set the temperature, flip occasionally, and come back when ready—it's the back and forth, action and reaction, between the cook and their creation offered with gas that sets it apart as a superior method both at home and the best restaurants in town.

And it's this type of difference that gets us to a theme that's been implicit throughout this book. Just as cooking with gas allows a chef to be more attentive, open, and interactive with their creations than in other modalities, skilled improvisation is both a foundational *philosophy* for the dimensions of an innovation culture and a *mindset* for practice.[1] As a philosophy, it underscores the responsiveness to changing people and situations at the heart of every effective enterprise. As a mindset, it provides an orientation for on-the-ground practice that lets ideas emerge generatively, collectively, and with fidelity to what's happening in the present.

In essence, as Heifetz, Grashow, and Linsky underscore, skilled improvisation is all about responding well to people in the current moment,

---

[1] For more on the improvisational mindset, see T.R. Dudeck, and C. McClure, eds. 2021. *The Applied Improvisation Mindset: Tools for Transforming Organizations and Communities* (New York, NY: Bloomsbury Publishing).

rather than constantly applying past beliefs or the templates in one's mind to what's happening in front of us.[2] For example, if a friend is telling you all about their amazing trip to the Grand Canyon and you immediately jump into the conversation with "I went to the Grand Canyon five years ago and didn't like it that much," you're making your experience (a past template in your head that you're slamming into the conversation) more important than empathetically listening to and being with your friend *in that moment*. In fact, many people go through their lives only applying the images or dictates in their heads to whatever's happening, without really taking in what's in front of them. Skilled improvisation makes one more attuned to sensing what's going on around you, to withholding judgment, to being curious about people, and, most of all, to sensing and responding to the shifts and flows of emotion and thought happening *now*. It's this philosophy and mindset that makes the art and science of building an innovation culture an improvisational undertaking.

An improvisational style is consistent with situational forms of leadership. Paul Hersey and Ken Blanchard's situational theory of leadership suggests that effective leaders are highly adaptive to the needs of the individuals they are leading, using different strategies according to the tasks being performed and the skill level and motivation of the employee.[3] In essence, situational leadership calls for leaders to wear multiple hats and never get stuck in one style—they must shift their styles by sometimes providing direction and sometimes stepping back to let others self-manage. But wait, doesn't improvisation mean doing just whatever comes to mind, flying by the seat of your pants, and making things up as you go along? Actually, no—and this is why it's critical to see what we mean by improvisation—so stick with us in dropping your assumptions for a moment about whatever you currently think the term means. Compared to "winging it" (what comes to mind for many people), skilled improvisation is "a highly-refined system of observing, connecting and responding" with

---

[2] R. Heifetz, A. Grashow, and M. Linsky. 2010. *The Practice of Adaptive Leadership: Tools and Tactics for Changing Your Organization and the World* (Cambridge: Harvard University Business Press), 195, p. 275.

[3] P. Hersey, and K. Blanchard. 1969. "An Introduction to Situational Leadership," *Training and Development Journal* 23, pp. 26–34.

other people.[4] That's it. If you've ever seen an improvisational comedy performance such as the television show *Whose Line Is It Anyway?*, it's the actors' ability to notice and respond well to one another that creates the conditions for an outstanding comedic performance. Although we think having a laugh together is a great goal and can create the conditions for a positive organization, what differs in terms of applied improvisation is that it's less about the humor and more about implementing that same general philosophy and mindset in our personal, professional, and organizational lives.[5]

So, what does this mean for the business leader hoping to create the conditions for an innovation culture? First, consider the astonishing connections between each of the main dimensions for innovation culture described in this book and improvisation. Let's name these links explicitly. *Collaboration* was the first dimension detailed in this book, and it simply can't be separated from improvisation. To collaborate well, one must work with others, and given the previous definitions, skilled improvisation requires attentiveness to groups. It's no solo act. To get there, seeing the world from others' perspectives and seeking to form emotional connections with them ground improvisation in acts of *empathy*. Yet each member of a business troupe needs to bring their own talents to the show, so to speak, and nothing sets the conditions for *personal creativity, diversity*, and personal, autonomous *freedoms* to flourish like a commitment to generative improvisation. With an improvisational philosophy and mindset, however, teams are best conceived with open, porous boundaries for *informal networks* to continually inform and reform an organization's efforts, as opposed to closed, self-sealing systems where no inputs from others are available.

---

[4] J. Bernard, and P. Short. 2015. *Jill and Patrick's Small Book of Improv for Business* (Portland, OR: Viewers Like You), p. 7.

[5] A global network of practitioners and scholars have formed the Applied Improvisation Network, of which Sanjay and Don are both a part. The network seeks to elevate the theories and practices of improvisation outside of theatrical settings in the way that we're describing in this chapter. See www .appliedimprovisationnetwork.org.

In fact, this is what it means to have an *innovation focus, flexibility*, and *market orientation*—skilled improvisers are relentlessly focused outward.[6] They consciously commit to the improvisational mindset by attending to what's happening around them. If competitors start moving their businesses further into digital spaces, they monitor those moves and react accordingly, as opposed to remaining static in the face of changing circumstances. To do so, they set up strategic internal *processes* (much like the structures of games that improvisational comedians play) that are outcomes focused. Overall, just as actors in an improvisational group need rehearsal spaces and physical objects such as chairs—or to follow our running analogy, just as cooks need pots, pans, ladles, and other equipment to cook—none of this can come about without investing significant *resources* to shifting the organization's culture in an innovative direction.

Second, what can really bring what we're describing into view is what Anil Jambekar and Karol I. Pelc call the difference between a "traditional mindset" and an "improvisation-based mindset."[7] In the former, for example, minor errors are "ignored or tolerated," but in the latter organizations see an "opportunity to create a novel solution." As further differences, the traditional mindset limits itself to the immediate context and similar others, while the improvisational mindset is focused on "continually expanding [one's/the group's] network regardless of functional skills and experience." Where the traditional mindset looks at resources from a deficit perspective: "we can't do this unless we have more of __ and __," the improviser says, "we can use what we have." It's probably the approach to learning that most separates these two very different ways of approaching business.

Where traditionalists focus on what Chris Agyris calls "single-loop" learning that stays within the routines of past thinking and procedures, improvisational actors make sure "double-loop" learning guides their actions, or learning that continually looks to form and reform,

---

[6] K. Leonard, and T. Yorton. 2015. *Yes, and: How Improvisation Reverses "No, but" Thinking and Improves Creativity and Collaboration* (New York, NY: Harper).
[7] A.B. Jambekar, and K.I. Pelc. October 2007. "Improvisation Model for Team Performance Enhancement in a Manufacturing Environment," *Team Performance Management: An International Journal*, 270.

dynamically rather than statically, the knowledge bases from which an organization operates.[8] It's the difference between Peter and David's approaches to innovation culture. One organization was stuck in past routines and policies that limited opportunity, while the other organization had porous boundaries, continually learning from and responding to shifts in competitors, audiences, and more. If there's anything we might sum this up to, it's that skilled improvisation uses structures that can bring about spontaneity, but also allows spontaneity to inform structures. That's the essence of innovation.

And we wouldn't want anyone reading this book to get the idea that by applied improvisation, we only mean what individuals do. Consistent with building a culture of innovation, an improvisational philosophy and mindset can be viewed from the standpoint of the organization itself. Stephen Leybourne finds that we're all now in a context of environmental turbulence, organizational responsiveness, service, and product life cycles being shortened, and "increasingly sophisticated, demanding, knowledgeable, and discerning customers."[9] Citing work by Stacey and Weick, Leybourne underscores how:

> Put simply, we as consumers want more choices, better quality, faster and more convenient delivery, and all at a lower price! This requires significant change on the part of traditional organizations, and we have seen a shift away from hierarchical, "command and control," micro-managed operational styles toward an organizational model based on "flattened" hierarchies, increased flexibility and local autonomy, the increased importance of inter and intra-organizational networks, of and self-directed, self-designed work. However, such a radical shift in organizational "style" also requires

---

[8] Jambekar and Pelc, 270; C. Agyris. September 1977. "Double Loop Learning in Organizations," *Harvard Business Review.* https://hbr.org/1977/09/double-loop-learning-in-organizations.

[9] S.A. Leybourne. 2010. "Improvisation as a Way of Dealing with Ambiguity and Complexity," *Graziado Business Review* 13, no. 3. https://gbr.pepperdine.edu/2010/08/improvisation-as-a-way-of-dealing-with-ambiguity-and-complexity-3/.

major changes in the way in which culture, motivation, commitment, and trust are addressed. Essentially, work is becoming less
"formalized," more "complex," and more "improvisational."[10]

As part of building what he terms an "improvisational ecology" (which
we see as "a culture of innovation"), Leybourne highlights that entire
industries can be thought about in terms of two improvisational qual-
ities: their creativity and analytical adaptability. Industries meeting the
demands of high creativity are those where assumptions need to be called
into question (much like double-loop learning) to meet rapid changes and
challenges, such as in many pharmaceutical companies. Think about the
challenge met in developing the Covid vaccine, for instance, where high
creativity was demanded to meet a pressing schedule. On the other hand,
with analytical adaptability, the techniques and tools used may need to
be amended or completely updated to meet the demands of the moment.
Software companies that continually seek to think through innovative
designs and technologies for accomplishing different ends have a high
degree of analytical adaptability. An example of low creativity and low
analytical adaptability would be straightforward IT maintenance, where
known protocols are simply implemented without much innovation or
attention to shifts in internal and external environments.[11] In each of
these ways, improvisation isn't simply a nice addition to what a business
or industry is up to but is in fact utterly at the core of carrying that
business or industry into a viable and productive future. All to say, as a
philosophy and mindset to be practiced, we ignore skilled improvisation
at great risk.

Finally, this book's second author wrote a book providing an A-to-Z
curriculum of both concepts and practices for training people in applied
improvisation, *Improv for Democracy: How to Bridge Differences and
Develop the Communication and Leadership Skills Our World Needs.*[12] Don

---

[10] Leybourne. n.d. "Improvisation," no. 4–5.

[11] Leybourne, "Improvisation."

[12] D. Waisanen. 2020. *Improv for Democracy: How to Bridge Differences and
Develop the Communication and Leadership Skills Our World Needs* (Albany, NY:
State University of New York Press).

grounded his project in the idea that we all have "default settings."[13] Both at individual and organizational levels, we all get stuck in routine patterns of action and interaction that are there because they served us well at some point. But when they become chronic, an improvisational approach is needed. For instance, if an angry employee stomps into a business owner's office upset about the lack of a forthcoming holiday bonus, and the owner reacts by getting mad at the employee, that response may simply reflect the owner's default setting for responding in kind in conflict situations. Better would be to break off that "default setting" and have other tools at hand—listening to and affirming the employees' concerns, taking in the message, and finding other, nonfinancial ways the staff might be compensated this year, and more. When we're stuck in our default settings, we too often fail to be present with others and adapt well to what's happening, which *requires* an improvisational approach.

Besides everything we have discussed in this book thus far on building a culture of innovation, some concepts and actions from this project can offer further insights.[14] One is "reacting to create," which is the idea that an improvisational approach to innovation often involves looking outside oneself for great sources of inspiration, rather than trying to invent products and services oneself. Sparks of inspiration are all around us if we're willing to look and listen attentively. Another concept is "repeating trust," or just the idea that those who engage in frequent and trust-filled communication will build supportive and inclusive cultures where innovation can thrive. The literatures supporting this concept are broad and deep and need to find their way into more workplaces. The concept of "advancing the ensemble" conceives of groups not simply as teams (drawing from the sports metaphor) but as theatrical collectives in which everyone leads where appropriate and is willing to step back when appropriate. As both Sanjay and Don have seen in many improvisational performance spaces, the saying "I've got your back" defines the ensemble approach. Other ideas with relevance include "improvising in liminality" (looking forward to and being comfortable in spaces of ambiguity and unpredictability),

---

[13] See Heifetz, Grashow, and Linsky, 178.

[14] All the quoted concepts in this paragraph are from Waisanen. *Improv for Democracy.*

facilitating cocreation (seeing creativity in terms of group activity at every opportunity), "improvising up and down the system" (never getting stuck in any one part of an organization but continually oscillating between macro and micro perspectives, from as many peoples' viewpoints as possible), and "fusing tasks with relationships" (never losing sight of the importance of setting tasks and objectives to be reached, while building relationships that fuel the fire for performance, and vice versa).

Overall, we'd feel remiss as we get closer to finishing this book without mentioning just how much power resides in conscious attention to improvisation. We'd go so far as to say that there's probably no other superpower more needed now for companies of all sizes. In a "volatile, uncertain, complex, and ambiguous" world especially, skilled improvisation is a philosophy and mindset that no organization seeking to be innovative can do without.[15] Yet, because no organization does what it does in a vacuum, it's also worth setting our sights on some larger happenings with relevance to building a culture of innovation, to which we now turn.

---

[15] N. Horney, B. Pasmore, and T. O'Shea. 2010. "Leadership Agility: A Business Imperative for a VUCA World," *People & Strategy* 33, no. 4, p. 34.

CHAPTER 20

Cooking in a Larger Context

Societies, Organizations, and Leadership

While skilled improvisation is fundamental to creating an innovative culture, there are also many connections between the themes covered in this book and cutting-edge work on societies, organizations, and leadership. Going back to our soup analogy, we are talking about the very nature of the community, restaurant, and its administration, each of which affect the quality of the soup. It's worth taking a moment to look further outward to the incredible new work that has developed across literatures, to see the role that building a culture of innovation can play in improving our world.

First, from a big picture perspective, the dimensions of innovation soup all play into what's been called the extraordinarily demanding "4th Industrial Revolution."[1] From technological revolutions in artificial intelligence to problems around climate justice, it's hard to keep pace with a world spinning with so many changes and challenges. The World Economic Forum highlights that, with "the acceleration of innovation and the velocity of disruption,"

> [I]n its scale, scope, and complexity, the transformation will be unlike anything humankind has experienced before. We do not yet know just how it will unfold, but one thing is clear: the response to it must be integrated and comprehensive, involving

---

[1] A. Bonime-Blanc. 2019. *Gloom to Boom: How Leaders Transform Risk Into Resilience and Value* (New York, NY: Routledge).

all stakeholders of the global polity, from the public and private sectors to academia and civil society.[2]

These developments highlight the need for skilled improvisation and a strategic responsiveness with customers and other stakeholders. Andrea Bonime-Blanc also finds that this is the fastest period of change human beings have ever confronted, where "no single genius or group of geniuses are capable of even getting their collective brains around everything that is coming at us," so new norms for "collaborative groups of virtual and actual cross-disciplinary experts" and others will need to work together to solve the planet's most pressing issues.[3]

In this environment, the demands for innovation and creativity have increased exponentially. To tackle these developments, as Albert Einstein put it, "We can't solve problems by using the same kind of thinking we used when we created them."[4] This is why many thinkers have argued for shifting our lenses from traditional business as usual operations to ideas like "the purpose economy," where morality, meaning, and collective approaches can infuse all aspects of individual, organizational, and societal life.[5] This is yet another difference between Peter and David's

---

[2] K. Schwab. January 14, 2016. "The Fourth Industrial Revolution: What It Means, How to Respond," *World Economic Forum*. www.weforum.org/agenda/2016/01/the-fourth-industrial-revolution-what-it-means-and-how-to-respond/.

[3] A. Bonime-Blanc. n.d. *Gloom to Boom* 252, p. 33; Horney, Pasmore, and O'Shea. n.d. "Leadership Agility," p. 34. This also means that elevating the type of training staff undergo should rise to a "civic" level in this day and age. See D.J. Waisanen. 2019. "Communication Training's Higher Calling: Using a Civic Frame to Promote Transparency and Elevate the Value of Services," In J.D. Wallace and D. Becker, eds., *Handbook of Communication Training* (New York, NY: Routledge), pp. 21–35.

[4] D. Mielach. April 19, 2012. "We Can't Solve Problems By Using The Same Kind Of Thinking We Used When We Created Them," *Business News Daily*. www.businessinsider.com/we-cant-solve-problems-by-using-the-same-kind-of-thinking-we-used-when-we-created-them-2012-4.

[5] A. Hurst. 2018. *The Purpose Economy* (U.S.: Imperative), front book cover; A. Dignan. 2019. *Brave New Work: Are You Ready to Reinvent Your Organization?* (New York, NY: Penguin).

approaches to building innovation culture—where one business leader finds themselves stuck in habits that worked well at one time, but have now become ill suited to contemporary demands, while the other sees ideating together, employee development, and organizational well-being as central drivers for productive and novel solutions. Overall, we're all in a situation where more and better collaboration is required to rise to the level of challenges wrought by this new wave in human connectedness and output, making the development of solidly innovative organizational cultures a necessity.

Second, how organizations are structured is no small matter, given these societal developments. Beyond examples previously presented in this book, such as holacracy, a great deal of thought and practice has gone into what it takes to move organizations from simple functional machines to outstanding spaces for innovation. Frédéric Laloux says we can think of organizations along an evolutionary scale.[6] At the bottom of this scale are "red" organizations that run on power and fear, with hierarchal authority and clear divisions of labor. Gangs and militias operate at this lowest level of organizational evolution. In the mid-range of development are "orange" organizations that run on competition and meritocracy, such as large corporations or universities. At some point, everyone has likely found themselves within this type of bureaucratic organization and, from the story told throughout this book, it's exactly the kind of organization David both inherited and managed. At the highest, most aspirational level, however, are what Laloux calls "teal" organizations that value collective and distributed decision making, self-management, continuous learning, and an incredible responsiveness to employees' needs and external shifts in real time.[7] Others have described such organizations' operating systems as "complexity conscious" and "people positive" and grounded in variables such as "trust"

---

[6] F. Laloux. 2014. *Reinventing Organizations: A Guide to Creating Organizations Inspired by the Next Stage in Human Consciousness* (Brussels, Belgium: Nelson Parker).

[7] Laloux. *Reinventing Organizations*; a clear visual for Laloux's overall scheme has been drawn from and can be found here: https://enliveningedge.org/views/reinventing-management-part-1-what-color-is-your-organization/.

and "psychological safety."[8] Connected with the work of Patrick Lencioni, these organizations build stellar teams by tending to results, making themselves accountable, committing to clear communal objectives, surfacing conflict, and creating safe, trustful spaces to have voice, as opposed to the practices of dysfunctional teams that forward poor performance, high turnover, the repetition of mistakes, little honesty about problems, and a fear of speaking up.[9] Like Peter's company, teal organizations are like "living organisms" and have the dimensions of innovation soup baked into their very DNA. Extending the analogy, they are innovative, "starfish" organizations whose internal dynamics are such powerful grounds for innovation that if one leg is cut off, not

---

[8] A. Dignan. n.d. *Brave New Work*; Edmondson, cited in Duhigg, "What Google Learned from Its Quest to Build the Perfect Team"; A.C. Edmondson. 2019. *The Fearless Organization: Creating Psychological Safety in the Workplace for Learning, Innovation, and Growth* (Hoboken, NJ: Wiley). For those working on diversity, equity, inclusion, and antiracism initiatives in and across organizations, we'd also add that the type of innovation described in this book can also have a decolonizing goal. With the objective of elevating voices across an organization while honing in on the importance of identities and the collective, there's much about working toward the status of "teal" organizations that connects with these purposes. Some goals should be, to borrow Tiara R. Na'puti's words, "to interrupt erasure and the logic of elimination embedded in enduring colonial violence—the goal is to denaturalize settler colonialism," as "a radical reimagining of kinships among land, people, the state—as a process as much as a goal," as actions that require "conversation and unlearning." D. Wanzer-Serrano, S.K. Sowards, V.N. Pham, G.A. Asante, and T.R. Na'puti. 2019. "Rhetoric's 'Distinguished' pitfalls: A plática," *Quarterly Journal of Speech* 105, no. 4, pp. 504–505. In this light, meeting the demands of the 4th Industrial Revolution should be positioned at the level of what organizations do, how they operate from within and without, and as a project dedicated to overcoming centuries of injustice at the core of many of the world's largest problems.

[9] P. Lencioni. 2006. *The Five Dysfunctions of a Team* (Hoboken, NJ: Wiley). See also J. Palfrey on the need to build both "safe" and "brave" spaces. J. Palfrey. 2018. *Safe Spaces, Brave Spaces: Diversity and Free Expression in Education* (Cambridge, MA: MIT Press).

only will a new leg grow back, but the old one will become an entirely new starfish.[10]

While they may not use the language of "teal" organizations (again, what we'd describe as organizations that are cranking on all cylinders with the dimensions of innovation culture), many thinkers have explained in detail what also goes into highly developed organizations. For those concerned about efficiency, these are organizations that strip out the most wasteful activities employees engage in when they show up to work. This should seem like an obvious point, but simply being in an organization from 9 a.m. to 5 p.m. does not equal important work getting done. The revolution in remote work forced by the Covid-19 pandemic more than proved that point—many people around the world found they were more productive working from home than slogging back and forth to a brick-and-mortar institution via train, bus, or car every day.

As Robert Kegan and Lisa Laskow Lahey highlight, many people show up to work and take on a second job much of the day: "spending time and energy covering up their weaknesses, managing other people's impressions of them, showing themselves to their best advantage, playing politics, hiding their inadequacies, hiding their uncertainties, hiding their limitations."[11] Over time, we also know that leaders tend to give their attention and resources to some employees while ignoring others, creating subtle patterns of inclusion and exclusion that can split an organization in two.[12] This can be highly demotivating for an organization and its

---

[10] In Brafman and Beckstrom's spider and starfish analogy, "If you cut off a spider's head, it dies; but if you cut off a starfish's leg, it grows a new one, and that leg can grow into an entirely new starfish. Traditionally, top-down organizations are like spiders, but now starfish organizations are changing the face of business and the world." O. Brafman, and R.A. Beckstrom. 2006. *The Starfish, and the Spider: The Unstoppable Power of Leaderless Organizations* (New York, NY: Penguin), synopsis.

[11] R. Kegan, and L.L. Lahey. 2016. *An Everyone Culture: Becoming a Deliberately Developmental Organization* (Harvard University Business Press: Boston), 1.

[12] F.C. Lunenburg. 2010. "Leader-Member Exchange Theory: Another Perspective on the Leadership Process," *International Journal of Management, Business, and Administration* 13, no. 1, pp. 1–5.

innovation.[13] All of these forces work against the transparency, account-ability, and elevation of individual and collective strengths in a culture of innovation. What this puts on the table is that every organization needs a *plan* to shift from wasteful defaults to the type of framework we've offered in this book, where everyone is engaged and creating value.

Third, innovation soup connects with the voluminous literature on leadership. People and organizations that give little thought into what goes into great leadership leave far too much to chance. One exercise Don likes to run in some of his classes involves getting students to list the qual-ities of the best and worst bosses they have ever had. This is not an exercise that anyone hems and haws about. Everyone has something to say about their experiences with good and bad leadership. The driving question is: What makes a good leader? We'd argue that each of the dimensions of innovation soup provide a structural foundation for the exercise of great leadership. Organizations that ground themselves in the dimensions will be way ahead of the curve in providing the very places and spaces most needed to do so. They create what Lev Vygotsky called a "Zone of Proxi-mal Development" or "the distance between the actual development level as determined by independent problem solving, and the level of potential development as determined through problem solving, under guidance or in collaboration with more capable peers."[14] Through norms of collabora-tion and informal networking, for instance, expectations can be set that anyone can step into a leadership role—that what an organization does is less about one great person than how a network of people have structured themselves to begin with. And this is what contemporary literature on leadership most pinpoints: leading with "we" rather than "me," fostering distributed learning, and putting the onus for leadership on the collective over and above individual contributions.[15]

---

[13] Our thanks go to Shekhar Mitra for this reaction and insight.

[14] Cited in L. Holzman. 2017. *Vygotsky at Work and Play* (New York, NY: Routledge), pp. 27–28.

[15] P. Cecchi-Dimeglio. May 18, 2020. "In Times of Anxiety, Lead With 'We' and 'Us'," *MIT Sloan Management Review*. https://sloanreview.mit.edu/article/in-times-of-anxiety-lead-with-we-and-us/; R. Men. April 16, 2020. "Leading in Wartime: 5 Ways CEOs Should Communicate With Their Workers Dur-

One type of leadership most crucial to our current moment is "leadership standpoints."[16] Standpoints refer to the many ways of looking at any issue and the many different people who should be spoken to on a continual basis, with an eye toward addressing the power imbalances, material constraints, and systemic inequalities that easily develop in organizations. While innovation soup describes the critical dimensions needed for innovation to flourish across an organization, leadership standpoints look to

---

ing Coronavirus," *UF College of Journalism and Communications.* www.jou.ufl.edu/insights/leading-in-wartime-5-ways-ceos-should-communicate-with-their-workers-during-coronavirus/; See P. Gronn. 2002. "Distributed Leadership as a Unit of Analysis," *The Leadership Quarterly* 13, no. 4, pp. 423–451; C.L. Pearce, and J.A. Conger. 2002. *Shared Leadership: Reframing the Hows and Whys of Leadership* (Thousand Oaks, CA: Sage); S. Gagnon, H.C. Vough, and R. Nickerson. 2012. "Learning to Lead, Unscripted: Developing Affiliative Leadership through Improvisational Theatre," *Human Resource Development Review* 11, no. 3, pp. 299–325; U. Stephan, M. Patterson, C. Kelly, and J. Mair. 2016. "Organizations Driving Positive Social Change: A Review and an Integrative Framework of Change Processes," *Journal of Management* 42, no. 5, pp. 1250–1281. There are also lots of ideas about practices like "participative management." M. Rolková, and V. Farkašová. 2015. "The Features of Participative Management Style," *Procedia Economics and Finance* 23, pp. 1383–1387. The differences that have been noted between leadership and management may also prove useful here: "Managers embrace process, seek stability and control, and instinctively try to resolve problems quickly—sometimes before they fully understand a problem's significance. Leaders, in contrast, tolerate chaos and lack of structure and are willing to delay closure in order to understand the issues more fully. . . .. leaders have much more in common with artists, scientists, and other creative thinkers than they do with managers. Organizations need both managers and leaders to succeed but developing both requires a reduced focus on logic and strategic exercises in favor of an environment where creativity and imagination are permitted to flourish." A. Zaleznik. 2004. "Managers and Leaders: Are They Different?" *Harvard Business Review*, para. 2. https://hbr.org/2004/01/managers-and-leaders-are-they-different. Further dimensions of management practice can be found in R.B. Denhardt, J.V. Denhardt, M.P. Aristigueta, and K.C. Rawlings. 2018. *Managing Human Behavior in Public and Nonprofit Organizations* (Thousand Oaks, Sage). For a comprehensive and quick overview of the range of theories about leadership, see K. Grint. 2010. *Leadership: A Very Short Introduction* (New York, NY: Oxford University Press).

[16] Waisanen, *Leadership Standpoints.*

specific practices those leading organizations can use as parallel to this project—namely, "practicing inclusion, building spaces for performance, and thinking and acting with range."[17]

Once again, the demands of the 4th Industrial Revolution are especially relevant. If we're to tackle the world's greatest challenges moving forward, we simply can't be on autopilot with our leadership philosophies and behaviors. In this revolution, "the most consequential and devastating risks are the risks of bad leadership," and in particular,

> leaders and organizations that do not amplify their lens to incorporate the views, risks and opportunities and consequences of ignoring (or even damaging) their full spectrum of key stakeholders . . . run the risk of losing to competitors, engaging in misadventures, increasing reputation risk, liabilities and losses or even losing their license to operate.[18]

Greatest among these is the need for practices of inclusion too long promised but too seldom offered in practice. In this book's terms, organizations must embrace the needs for diversity, collaboration, informal networks, resource distributions, and the offering of creativity to more people in more places than ever before.

This means that leaders should work to understand the contexts and codes that include or exclude working for both the unity and diversity possible within an innovative organization.[19] They should "zoom in" and

---

[17] Waisanen, *Leadership Standpoints.*

[18] Bonime-Blanc. n.d. *From Gloom to Boom* 42, p. 25; See also M. Uhl-Bien, R. Marion, and B. McKelvey. August 2007. "Complexity Leadership Theory: Shifting Leadership from the Industrial Age to the Knowledge Era," *The Leadership Quarterly* 18, no. 4, pp. 298–318.

[19] For example, Arya Gray argues that, indeed, "Professionalism has become coded language for white favoritism in workplace practices that more often than not privilege the values of white and Western employees and leave behind people of color." A. Gray. June 04, 2019. "The Bias of 'Professionalism' Standards," *Stanford Social Innovation Review.* https://ssir.org/articles/entry/the_bias_of_professionalism_standards#. The focus on culture also aligns with much literature arguing for strategic rather than reactive approaches to the subject; See, for

"zoom out," or alternate between being on the "dance floor" and the "balcony."[20] We often think of Carl Sagan's humbling "pale blue dot" speech with this kind of leadership. Sagan referred to photos of earth from afar to underscore the "very small stage in a vast cosmic arena" humans work within, which should put every leader's grand ambitions in a humbling frame of reference.[21] It is important to have leadership that cultivates learning from failure. Top leaders need to do this by taking responsibility for success and failure as the P&G example discussed.

Businesses grounded in empathy, a cornerstone of "emotional intelligence" theory, will put their focus outside of themselves to stay attentive to how people feel and not just think about their products and services.[22] And, consistent with the findings in this project, emotional intelligence

---

instance, D.D. Warrick. May–June 2017. "What Leaders Need to Know About Organizational Culture," *Business Horizons* 60, no. 3, pp. 395–404; L. Dreier, D. Nabarro, and J. Nelson. September 24, 2019. "Systems Leadership Can Change the World—But What Exactly is It?" *World Economic Forum.* www.weforum .org/agenda/2019/09/systems-leadership-can-change-the-world-but-what-does-it-mean/. It's critical to note that "Leadership development is context-sensitive. There is no one best way to lead or to develop leaders. In different settings, there may be different expectations of leaders and different practices that make them effective." It's "an ongoing process. . . grounded in personal [and collective] development, which is never complete." McCauley, Velsor, and Ruderman. n.d. 3, p. 26. P.G. Northouse. 2015. *Leadership: Theory and Practice* (Thousand Oaks: Sage), adapted from P.W. Dorfman, P.J. Hanges, and F.C. Brodbeck. 2004. "Leadership and Cultural Variation: The Identification of Culturally Endorsed Leadership Profiles," In *Culture, Leadership, and Organizations: The GLOBE Study of 62 Societies,* eds. R.J. House, P.J. Hanges, M. Javidan, P.W. Dorfman, and V. Gupta (Thousand Oaks, CA: Sage), pp. 669–719.

[20] R.M. Kanter. March 2011. "Managing Yourself: Zoom In, Zoom Out," *Harvard Business Review.* https://hbr.org/2011/03/managing-yourself-zoom-in-zoom-out, pars. 3–4; Heifetz, Grashow, and Linsky. n.d. *The Practice of Adaptive Leadership,* 7.

[21] Pale Blue Dot—30th Anniversary | National Geographic. February 14, 2020. *National Geographic / Youtube.* www.youtube.com/watch?v=hKFkR9yfRoY. *Note that the former link does not work, but this could be a possible new citation with video link that works: Cool Worlds, "Pale Blue Dot 2020," YouTube, February 13, 2020. www.youtube.com/watch?v=qDjiSc_J3Ac.

[22] D. Goleman. 2006. *Emotional Intelligence* (New York, NY: Bantam).

isn't the only kid on the block anymore. "Cultural intelligence" constitutes an equally if not more important variable that's been developed out in a wealth of scholarship. The variable stands as a separate competency from emotional intelligence as practices for leaders to pursue.[23] And different cultural ways of leading itself become a lens that promotes organizational diversity, such as thinking about the effects that one's leadership will have seven generations from now.[24] Such "*worldly* leadership" should be part and parcel of the innovation soup we've described in this book[25]

---

[23] See D. Livermore. 2015. *Leading With Cultural Intelligence* (New York, NY: AMACOM).

[24] J. Bordas. 2012. *Salsa, Soul, and Spirit: Leadership for a Multicultural Age* (Oakland, CA: Berrett-Koehler). "What is the Seventh Generation Principle?" *Indigenous Corporate Training*, May 29, 2012, www.ictinc.ca/blog/seventh-generation-principle; See also "What is Servant Leadership?" Robert K. Greenleaf Center for Servant Leadership, 2016. www.greenleaf.org/what-is-servant-leadership/; A. Arora, M. Elawar, and S. Cheng. 2019. "Socially Conscious Leadership: An Integrated Model," *Journal of Leadership Studies* 13, no. 3, p. 38. What's clear is that "what works well in one organization, culture, or country, may well produce failure in another organization, culture, or country;" G. Jacobs, A. Van Witteloostuijn, and J. Christe-Zeyse. 2013. "A Theoretical Framework of Organizational Change," *Journal of Organizational Change Management* 26, no. 5, p. 775. Further focusing how leadership cannot be culture and gender neutral, Roya Ayman and Karen Korabik describe some factors making up the "labyrinth" that women and other leaders face: "stereotypes and schemes, ingroup-outgroup dynamics, role expectations, power and status differentials, and differential attributions made about, and rewards given for similar behavior." R. Ayman, and K. Korabik. 2010. "Leadership: Why Gender and Culture Matter," *American Psychologist* 65, no. 3, p. 157. Judy Rosesner also argues that masculine styles tend to be grounded in "transactional leadership," whereas feminine styles tend to be more oriented toward "transformational" and "interactive leadership." J.B. Rosener. November–December 1990. "Ways Women Lead," *Harvard Business Review*, pars 6–8. https://hbr.org/1990/11/ways-women-lead.

[25] Fitting with the demands of the 4th Industrial Revolution, worldly leadership has been described as "a pooling of the combined leadership wisdoms from all parts of the globe—whether these are contemporary or ancient wisdoms. We fear that as the world becomes increasingly homogenous as a result of the 'flattening' impact of the internet and advancing global communication technology, the existing dominant voices may drive out the leadership wisdoms of minority,

and fit with the direction of Peter's company, as an organization committed to all the ingredients of the innovation soup—especially in building informal networks, advancing diversity, and building spaces and processes for collaboration that involve different people at all leadership levels.

Skilled contemporary leaders further build spaces where human beings' needs for autonomy, mastery, and purpose can flourish,[26] manage the energy flows within an organization, not just time,[27] and make conversations and transformative, positive communication central drivers for

---

indigenous and ancient wisdoms. It does not have to be so. With . . . new technologies, an opportunity now presents itself for leaders across the world to share and combine the leadership knowledge and practice that exist in many corners of the world: wisdoms that would otherwise remain unknown outside their community. Ancient philosophies can enable us to reframe and rethink the enormous challenges of responsible, ethical, and sustainable leadership of the world. The majority of leaders across the globe today have been conditioned in some way by western and US-centric leadership theories and methodologies. This thinking has been driven through our global business schools and business cultures, often to the exclusion of non-western traditions and cultures and the valuable insights and wisdom these may have to offer." P. Case, S. Turnbull, and S. Khakwani. 2012. "Introduction: The Emerging Case for Worldly Leadership," In *Worldly Leadership: Alternative Wisdoms for a Complex World*, eds. S. Turnbull, P. Case, G. Edwards, D. Schedlitzki, and P. Simpson (London, UK: Palgrave Macmillan), p. 3.

[26] D. Pink. 2011. *Drive: The Surprising Truth about What Motivates Us* (New York, NY: Riverhead). We'd also add that seeing the possibilities for employees to grow and change is critical to this perspective. One of the most enduring, problematic notions in popular culture is of "hard-wiring." Countering this is "neural plasticity," since, "with the possible exception of inborn reflexes, remarkably few psychological capacities in humans are genuinely hard-wired, that is, inflexible in their behavioral express. . . . Moreover, virtually all psychological capacities, including emotions and language, are modifiable by environmental experiences." S.O. Lilienfeld, K.C. Sauvigné, S.J. Lynn, R.L. Cautin, R.D. Latzman, and I.D. Waldman. 2015. "Fifty Psychological and Psychiatric Terms to Avoid: A List of Inaccurate, Misleading, Misused, Ambiguous, and Logically Confused Words and Phrases," *Frontiers in Psychology* 6, p. 4.

[27] T. Schwartz, and C. McCarthy. October 2017. "Manage Your Energy, Not Your Time," *Harvard Business Review*. https://hbr.org/2007/10/manage-your-energy-not-your-time.

theory and action.[28] They think broadly and make continuous learning a centerpiece of their organizational commitments.[29] Innovative leaders engage in design thinking and how they can shape environments that foster certain actions: the very soup we've described in this book. Elements such as architecture, lighting, seating, and more all impact human behaviors.[30] They'll pay attention to digital and remote ecologies as much as whatever else goes on at the physical office.[31]

And for a subject that is vastly focused on external tasks and relationships, leaders should also give conscious attention to taking care of and developing themselves. You're no good if burnt out all the time. Practices in mindfulness and connecting with the body can be critical to keeping leaders going during stress-filled and turbulent times.[32]

---

[28] A. Credi, and C. Ainsworth. December 10, 2019. "Transforming Your Culture With Conversations," *Center for Creative Leadership*. https://cclwebinars .webvent.tv/webinar/3545; J Mirivel. 2014. *The Art of Positive Communication: Theory and Practice* (New York, NY: Peter Lang). Great leaders also promote democratic discussion. See S.D. Brookfield, and S. Preskill. 2012. *Discussion as a Way of Teaching: Tools and Techniques for Democratic Classrooms* (San Francisco, CA: Jossey-Bass); J.M.G. Burns. 2004. *Transforming Leadership* (New York, NY: Grove Press).

[29] D. Epstein. 2019. *Range: Why Generalists Triumph in a Specialized World* (New York, NY: Penguin); K.S. Milway, and A. Saxton. 2011. "The Challenge of Organizational Learning," *Stanford Social Innovation Review*. https://ssir.org/ articles/entry/the_challenge_of_organizational_learning#.

[30] See, for example, A. Arieff. July 18, 2011. "Beyond the Cubicle," *The New York Times*. http://opinionator.blogs.nytimes.com/2011/07/18/beyond-the-cubicle/? hp; A. Alter. 2014. *Drunk Tank Pink: And Other Unexpected Forces that Shape How We Think, Feel, and Behave* (New York, NY: Penguin). See also L.G. Bolman, and T.E. Deal. 2017. *Reframing Organizations: Artistry, Choice, and Leadership* (San Francisco, CA: Jossey-Bass).

[31] As some have put it, an immaterial digital surface has now been placed upon almost every part of our planet's material surface. B. Alexander. 2017. *The New Digital Storytelling: Creating Narratives With New Media* (Santa Barbara, CA: Abc-clio).

[32] One great concept for this is the idea of using "purposeful pauses." J. Marturano. 2014. *Finding the Space to Lead: A Practical Guide to Mindful Leadership* (New York, NY: Bloomsbury). P. Hamill. 2013. *Embodied Leadership: The Somatic Approach to Developing your Leadership* (London, UK: Kogan Page Publishers);

At the end of the day, everyone brings to work each day a set of ideas about what leadership should look like, how organizations should operate, and their impacts on society. These ideas matter. Bad ideas about leadership can create low morale among employees and affect many bottom-line variables like retention. Poor ideas about organizations can lock people into tribal and unproductive ways of organizing themselves. Companies that are cut off from all that's going on in the world externally will fail to be responsive and reach their competitive potential.[33] It's thus now more important than ever to lay a groundwork for leadership, organizations, and societies that thrive. Using the dimensions and guidelines for innovation soup—that connect with many of the best ideas and practices that have emerged across fields—can put an organization on the path to excellence that all people want and deserve.

L.R. Melina, G.J. Burgess, L. Lid-Falkman, and A. Marturano, eds. 2013. *The Embodiment of Leadership* (San Francisco, CA: Jossey-Bass). Overall, "Research shows that the single biggest cause of work burnout is not work overload but working too long without experiencing your own personal development." Kegan and Lahey. n.d. *An Everyone Culture*, 2.

[33] John Maynard Keynes once summarized this perspective about how we all carry theories with us in our daily thoughts and actions: "The ideas of economists and political philosophers, both when they are right and when they are wrong, are more powerful than is commonly understood. Indeed, the world is ruled by little else. Practical men [*sic*], who believe themselves to be quite exempt from any intellectual influences, are usually the slaves of some defunct economist. Madmen in authority, who hear voices in the air, are distilling their frenzy from some academic scribbler of a few years back. I am sure that the power of vested interests is vastly exaggerated compared with the gradual encroachment of ideas. Not, indeed, immediately, but after a certain interval; for in the field of economic and political philosophy there are not many who are influenced by new theories after they are twenty-five or thirty years of age, so that the ideas which civil servants and politicians and even agitators apply to current events are not likely to be the newest." Cited in P. Krugman. March 05, 2011. "Madmen in Authority: An Update," *The New York Times*. https://krugman.blogs.nytimes.com/2011/05/05/madmen-in-authority-an-update/.

CHAPTER 21

Some Exercises to Fuel Innovation

Today's business leaders want their employees to help them invent creative, fresh solutions to their biggest problems. One way is to teach employees to think innovatively. In this chapter, we provide some concrete exercises to help you do exactly that, fueling innovation in your organization. You can think about these as tinder for the fire. They'll help start you on the path to many of the dimensions, while underscoring that there are several ways forward with building a culture for innovation. Almost all of these exercises work with the type of improvisational philosophy and mindset and connections with organizational, leadership, and societal literatures described in the previous two chapters.

In our interventions and work with clients, just like Laura, we do a deep dive and develop a programmatic approach based on the specific conditions, results, and requirements at the client end. Besides these, we also conduct general-purpose workshops and interventions that can help ignite an innovative mindset. These are workshops based on improvisational methods that get cross-functional teams together in one room (remotely or in-person). Next we provide some ideas and general guidelines on such workshops to give you a general sense of what the activities are and how they can help. Unlike the more concrete, company-specific interventions, these are intentionally more general for the purposes of this book. They are all also extremely flexible and customizable—to suit the specific purpose of your company. Once you get a sense of what they are, feel free to tweak and experiment as you see fit!

Getting Started

To get your team used to the idea of improvisation, and to develop the spirit of teamwork, open a session with warm-up exercises and short-form improv games before moving to more complex activities. One great warm-up is the "Shake-8." The session leader directs participants by shaking first the right hand eight times, then the left, followed by the right leg (knee raised) eight times and finally the left leg rapidly. All count out loud with each shake. The exercise is repeated with each limb as we go down to seven shakes, six shakes, all the way down to one. This quickly gets the blood flowing and team members more into their bodies and less in their heads. This is critical for removing frictions or tensions in the room or space, allowing free-flowing ideas to emerge.

Another warm-up is "Sun and Moon" in which participants stand in a circle and secretly pick one classmate as their sun and another as their moon.[1] When the game starts, all the participants move around as they try to put their suns between themselves and their moons. Since one person's sun could be another's moon, it's a fun free-for-all with a lot of movement. More importantly, it forces people to become alert, tuned in to their surroundings, and aware of the people nearby. One of the more profound aspects of the exercise can be highlighted by having a second round where you ask everyone in the room to go in "slow motion." In the second round, the slowing down allows everyone to replace their previously frenetic movements with a more considered, observational viewpoint on what's happening in the room. Participants will often report feeling a sense for both their parts and the whole in the second version, whereas they were mostly using their own viewpoints in the first. A great team command to use after this exercise is "let's slow down" to allow a more systemic and collaborative viewpoint to emerge.

Once everyone is warmed up, you can move on to a short game such as One-Word Story. As participants sit in a circle, one person is chosen to speak a word; the person beside her says another word, and the person beside him adds the next. The goal is to tell a coherent story one word at a time. This exercise is brilliant for teaching cocreation and building on

---

[1] See Waisanen, *Improv for Democracy*.

the resources of your teammates. An alternate version has everyone practice making "deep philosophical statements" with one another. These are one-sentence statements, again constructed one word at a time, which get the group to try to create profound sayings out of the ether. The laughter that usually ensues from this exercise is alone worth the effort.

Or you can play Emotional Symphony, in which one person is a conductor and four or five other people are assigned emotions. As the conductor points to the other players, they express their emotions through poses and noises, varying their intensity as the conductor's hand rises or falls. Following "Shake-8," this exercise is great for unlocking participants' energies and movement, putting both their minds and bodies in a state that's capable of being innovative and receptive to the innovations of others. Another possibility is Mirrors, in which pairs of participants take turns mimicking each other's movements. All these activities are designed to get participants thinking and acting in new ways.

Longer descriptions of these and a universe of other exercises can be found at learnimprov.com or improvencylopedia.com. To lay a foundation for practicing the dimensions of innovation culture, we encourage you to pick three improv exercises to carry out with your participants at the beginning of every session focused on innovation.

Shaping the Mind

Besides improv, as the team progresses on its journey toward unlocking the creative potential of the mind, we also introduce practices from guided visualization, yoga and meditation, and automatic drawing and writing.

Guided visualization. For this exercise, dim the lights and instruct participants to follow along to a voice prompt, which leads them through progressive relaxing of each of their muscle groups, starting with the face. Many sample videos can be found on YouTube.[2] This is an easy, low-stakes, approachable way for participants to relax and rejuvenate their minds as they slip into a meditative state, creating the conditions for innovation readiness.

---

[2] Youtube. February 08, 2013. Breathe With Me, "Guided Visualization Exercise." www.youtube.com/watch?v=awLHRRfeCUA&t=197s.

Yoga and mindfulness techniques. Up front, we treat both yoga and meditation in a scientific, secular, completely nonreligious manner as tools to help the mind and body. You can introduce participants to breathing exercises, basic yoga poses, and the underlying philosophy of yoga that is, like improvisation, grounded in getting everyone into a mindful and present-focused state of being. This gives participants insight into the importance of yoga and its connection with overall wellness. Simplify the process of meditation and emphasize that it is not a mystical practice. To use a metaphor, our minds are like the ocean with all stress and turbulence on the surface, while underneath the waves, there is stillness. Meditation helps us connect with this stillness. Evidence of the popularity of such techniques in corporate America can be found in the mushrooming of businesses such as Calm that proudly claims to have over 1,500 clients and has done wonders for creating the conditions for self-care and awareness that are critical to innovative work.[3]

Poet and author William Plomer said, "Creativity is the power to connect the seemingly unconnected." One of the reasons we recommend the use of meditation with your team is that it frees the mind to make those connections. Many times, our conscious minds are so busy with the rush of our day-to-day priorities that they do not allow us to see those connections (or, as the sun and moon exercise emphasized, the system at work), but meditation calms our thoughts, giving us the freedom to make unexpected associations that can spark innovative ideas.

Automatic drawing. This technique has been used in sessions involving everything from art to religion. Participants place their pens or pencils against blank sheets of paper, close their eyes, and let their dominant hands move around on the page as their conscious minds "lose control" of their actions. Encourage your staff to not look at their work or judge it in any way (and the preceding improv and meditative exercises are great for getting people into a mindset where judgments are minimized). Tell them: "You're the observer, not the controller. Don't dwell on any thoughts that come to your mind—just dismiss them and let them pass through. If necessary, tell yourself repeatedly, 'Whatever comes out is fine.'"

---

[3] "Home Page," Calm. www.calm.com/.

Eventually, your participants should set aside the first sheet without looking at it, then pick up a second sheet and start over. Once we stop the second experiment, the class is opened for discussion. We encourage participants to look at their squiggly lines and see if there's anything that surprises them or that they want to share with the class. Results vary widely among the participants and can lead to lively discussions.

Automatic writing. As a variation of automatic drawing, participants set their pens to blank paper and write whatever the hand suggests, without worrying about grammar, structure, spelling, or other restrictions. It needs to be noted though that, based on the experience of running these two individual exercises (automatic drawing and writing) over many years, the reactions can be variable.

Where you'll be on solid footing is conducting an improv- and team-based version of these exercises that involves creating a face among teams of four to five participants, with the rules that everyone must be silent and can only add one line to the drawing at a time. Put a big sheet of flip chart paper on the floor and have four to five people sit around each, with black markers available for each person. You can also add two eyeballs to each blank surface just to get everyone ready to draw a face together. When you say "go," give everyone about five minutes to draw one line of the face at a time (e.g., a circle for the outline of the face can be one line, the drawing of an eyebrow is one line). It's good to let everyone know that, while they should only be silent and not try to control what others add to the face, they are free to laugh just to release that motivating energy and create a positive climate. Once round one is completed, you can add a round two where everyone creates a name for the person they drew, one letter at a time. The exercise is not only hilarious but truly underscores the cocreative dimensions seen throughout this book. Another option is to have one representative from each group come up to introduce everyone to the person in the drawing. Framed as "we'd like to introduce you all to a new employee who will be joining our organization starting next week," it's amazing to see the creativity and energies that this exercise releases among all. Participants especially get to see a different side of each other and learn to trust that they can build together in ways previously not thought possible.

Empathy exercise. Participants are provided with sets of pictures that depict a few, diverse families living out their daily lives. Each participant is asked to pick one face and develop empathy toward that person. That is, imagine what that person's life is like and build a character and description of that individual. Provide your employees with a framework they can use and make it clear that the more nuanced their character description, the better. Participants must also identify one pressing need or "pain point" this person might have.

Next, the groups are randomly assigned to one of three different industries, which might be as disparate as food, transportation, software development, health care, or insurance. The groups should develop a product and marketing program that would help solve the pain points of the individuals for whom they have created empathetic relationships. Participants often tell us later that this exercise is the one that has helped them most as they work on other projects and presentations, and even as they go through job interviews. This empathy exercise is especially important for design thinking classes with their emphasis on thinking about user experiences, emotions, and the diverse lives of people across the world.

Advanced Improvisation

Yes–and. Once you've had a chance to get everyone warmed up and run through some of the shaping-the-mind meditations and other exercises, building on our experience with improv, we teach participants basic improv techniques such as yes–and, in which one person suggests an idea and the next person accepts the idea and builds on it (e.g., pose the question: Where should we go on vacation this year? Person A might say "Let's go to Munich." Person B would then say, "Yes, and let's take a business class flight there." Person A could then say, "Yes, and let's make sure to order the lobster for dinner on that flight." And so on. So long as each person says "Yes–and" at the start of their sentence they'll get the gist of this). These yes–and exercises initially start generally but gradually become more focused on business problems. (See the section titled "The book case" below for an example of a yes-and exercise we use in our classes.)

We then move on to more complicated activities. For instance, we give participants a list of five products and ask them to develop an ad for one of them, using the creativity techniques we have discussed in class. They must also document the creative process they used in the ad design—for instance, did they generate a distinct number of different ideas before settling on one? Thus, they are assessed not only on their results but also on their journey.

In a similar exercise, we first take participants through some of the basics of jingle writing. Participants are then given a choice of five brands and charged with writing lyrics and music for a jingle for one of the brands. As with the ad exercise, we assess participants on the process and the results.

To stimulate creativity under pressure, we finally leave participants in a busy shopping area on campus and give them two hours to come up with a concept for a restaurant. Because there are such tight time limits, for this assignment we only assess the product, not the process, which readies participants for a very results-focused pitch that forms the core for many successful business initiatives with investors and other stakeholders.

In fact, we have found that the session can be transformative. For instance, last year there was a participant who was initially skeptical of the yes–and method. When this participant realized that participants would go around in a circle to call out their ideas one by one, she said, "This means I have to patiently listen to all the stupid ideas before mine." Sanjay responded, "You seem to be prejudging your colleagues' comments, and we are trying to move away from judgment." This simple observation made her change her attitude, and she became the most enthusiastic participant in class.

PowerPoint karaoke. This exercise, which we've been running for years, focuses on participants' presentation skills. We put together five Power-Point decks with unconnected, randomly selected slides. These include irrelevant but impressive-looking data as well as some funny visuals. Groups are asked to come up to the podium one by one and "present" this deck as if they prepared it. The key is that they have no time to review them before they are asked to make a presentation. They are also asked to present with the same passion, enthusiasm, and energy they would muster for a presentation they *had* prepared. We also sometimes play the "clicker," which means how long a slide stays on depends on the facilitator—they must continue to build on it if it is on. Or you can run a version where the slides are timed at, say, 10 seconds each before moving on to the next. For well over a decade, this exercise, used in classes, workshops, and more, has never failed to build camaraderie, creative confidence, and presentation skills across countries and cultures in our classes and workshops.

The book case. Building on all that's come previously, tell everyone that they are part of the marketing team at Barnes & Noble. The chain has been experiencing declining sales for the past decade, in large part because Amazon has been selling books online at a significant discount. The CEO has pulled your team into the office to demand that you come up with marketing-based answers. You retire to the "marketing think-tank" and decide to use the yes–and exercise to devise a solution. Furthermore, you decide to play the game with post-it notes instead of verbally. This is how you will play:

1. One of you will be the initiator. That person will come to the center and say, "We should…" and propose a solution. Write this idea on a post-it note and paste it on the board. (*Note*: At this point, the ideas should be on a broad and general level, not full of specific nitty-gritty details. You can also do this exercise online using a Google Jamboard that allows participants to see and put post-it notes up in a single whiteboard space.)

2. The next person in the group will go to the center and say, "Yes! And…" and add to the original idea. Write this suggestion on a new post-it note and paste it on the board. Keep in mind, this is not about time pressure. Each participant can take 5 or 10 seconds to come up with the next yes–and idea.

3. Repeat this cycle until all group members have contributed.

4. At this point, the initiator can either call out "New Choice!" if they believe the group needs to go in a new direction, or "Build!" if they like the current ideas. The next group member now becomes the new initiator. If the first initiator has called for a new choice, the second initiator repeats the initial process, but takes the group in a different direction. The post-it notes should start on a different line, parallel to the first. If the choice is to build on an existing idea, the new initiator will repeat the original process, but dig deeper into some of the current ideas.

The post-it notes should branch off vertically, up, and down from the last note in the first round.

5. Any group member can initiate and play the part of initiator. After the last group member has added their idea, you stop the game and huddle together to discuss the web of post-it notes. You can make connections between notes, explore combinations, and consider other directions.

6. As a group, you should then determine whether anything meaningful came from your yes–and exercise. Present your ideas by filling out the five fields on a "solution" paper. You don't need to include a great deal of copy with any of the answers. You just need to present an idea that is strong, well thought-out, and implementable.

Our Solution

Finally, having gone through these exercises (or many others via the sites we have suggested), we encourage your group to get together at the end of each session to address each of the following prompts. Although your team exercise session may have focused on process and being open-ended, now is the time to engage in convergent thinking by bringing everyone together to focus on the next steps. Remember that creativity and innovation are different, in that the latter is very much about creating with outcomes or products in mind. Even if the exercises in this chapter were only a jump start for your group's thinking, any part of your process that might lead to productive or profitable outcomes should be collectively sifted through by the end of the meeting.

And we encourage you to think about a concept we have always found helpful: the idea of going for "15 percent solutions" that create small steps to change, rather than "100 percent solutions" that can paralyze thinking and action.[4] Even taking one step forward in building your culture of innovation can be a significant outcome if it helps put everyone in a state of being that readies employees for the challenges and opportunities ahead. But for now, go ahead and lead your team through each of the following prompts, and make sure to document all contributions created,

---

[4] See www.liberatingstructures.com/7-15-solutions/.

to be forwarded at your next meeting or translated directly to practice in your work.

What we should do:

Why we should do it:

How we should do it:

When we should do it:

What the outcome will likely be:

Epilogue

"25 years, David!"

"I know! They were fantastic years, Phil! I can't thank you enough for all those years of hard work," said David.

"I really don't have any other choice. I am sorry," said Phil.

They were seated in David's office, the same room on the c-suite corner of the fourth floor of the building that served as corporate headquarters for his company. A lot had changed in the past 10 years, but not everything. Now in his 60s, David still had the same tie, khaki pants, pressed shirt, and warm, effusive manner. He was liked and respected by his employees.

"Those were the exact words you had said to me that day 10 years ago, David. I can never forget them," said Phil.

"Except this time, it's you who is sorry and doesn't have a choice," said David. They both laughed heartily.

"I thoroughly enjoyed working for you David," said Phil. He meant it. He really liked David. He and Phil still shared a passion for beer. They would often head out after work to try out a new brewery.

"So have I Phil."

"But I gotta go now man," said Phil.

Phil had stopped by to announce his desire to retire; 10 years ago, on this very day, David had fired him. Phil's life had turned upside down that day. He thought he could never recover from that debacle. An entire year had passed without any worthwhile offers. He had decided it was better to wait than to accept a compromise offer, and then one day, the phone rang, and it was David who wanted him back.

"I still don't know why you hired me back 10 years ago," said Phil.

"Laura suggested that you would be a key member of the new, re-energized team," said David. "She believed your experience and knowledge were invaluable."

"But wasn't I a relic of the old ways? A dinosaur?"

"Laura knew it wasn't your fault Phil. She felt that a change in the culture of the company was needed. She did let some people go, but she also retained some of the wisdom," said David.

"She is amazing!" said Phil.

"She is. She helped me turn this company around Phil. I could not have done it without her."

"Well, I am glad you called me back. The last 10 years have been the best years of my professional life," said Phil.

"Are you sure I can't entice you to stay a little longer?" asked David.

"Thanks, but no thanks. I have things to do. My family needs me. I had planned on retiring at 60, you dragged me on until 65!" said Phil with a smile.

"It has been a pleasure Phil. Hey, I am meeting an old friend for drinks later. Care to join?" asked David.

"Can't tonight. Beth needs me; she has a doctor's appointment she can't drive back from."

"Well, you are here another week, let's get a drink soon," said David.

"Sure thing man," said Phil. "Door open or shut?" he asked politely, getting up to leave.

"My door is always open Phil, you know that," said David with a smile.

He was looking forward to drinks with Peter. They had made it an annual tradition to meet at Sol, the brewery, on this very evening. He had a lot to fill him on. He could never forget that evening 10 years ago when he and Peter had met for drinks. It had changed his life and his company. He had listened to Peter's advice and hired Laura who was instrumental in transforming his company. It was not easy, nor was it fast but, over time, he saw the change unfold in front of his eyes. He had had to let go of some people and bring back some but there was now a new culture in place. A culture in which innovation was a way of life. The Covid pandemic had lasted a while longer than he had hoped, but his company had worked around it.

He was humming a tune and getting ready to leave for his date with Peter when Peter texted that he was running late. His company was celebrating, and they needed him a bit longer.

"He is at it again!" thought David to himself with a smile. He decided to stick with his plans; he could always get a taster or two before Peter showed up. He called Steve, his car bot, to pick him up and made his way to the elevator (wonder why he named his bot Steve?). He had a couple of e-mails to respond to, but he could do that on his drive. Steve wouldn't mind; he was polite. He knew exactly where David needed to go—he was connected to David's organizer.

"I am so glad I don't have to drive," said David to himself as he made his way to his car. Steve had brought the car around and was waiting. He was always there, efficient, reliable, and invisible. It was 2032, no one drove. After all, innovation drives change.

Appendix

What the Scores Mean

InnoQ™ score: This is the aggregate score, combining scores across all employees, across all four questions for each of the 11 dimensions. This score indicates overall how *innovation ready* the organization is across all 11 dimensions.

Actual innovation: This comes from a separate set of six questions that employees answer pertaining to the actual innovation they have seen at their company—these questions pertain to items such as number of innovative ideas, products and initiatives, and historic innovation by the company and reputation.

Actual innovation regressed on InnoQ™ score: figure A.1 shows the relationship between InnoQ™ score and actual innovation. A strong relationship indicates that the InnoQ™ score is predictive of innovation.

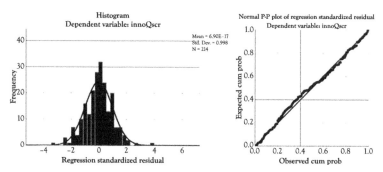

Figure A.1 Innovation regressed on InnoQ™ score

The regression coefficient is well above satisfactory. Companies that had overall high scores on all those 10 dimensions ended up in that top quartile and are also the most innovative.[1] This is across 24 industries. So,

---

[1] As mentioned earlier, there were only 10 dimensions at the time of this data collection.

what is new? First, these data provide hard evidence on the importance of innovation readiness. Secondly, built on the rigorous data collection and analysis, we now have a handy tool that can help organizations look under the hood and assess the company's innovation readiness or Innovation Quotient (InnoQ™).

Industry Analysis

When we collected data from individuals using the InnoQ™, we asked them their company name. We then coded each response into the appropriate industry (e.g., the responses from IBM were put into the "IT" category). In this way, we were able to identify the industry that each of the responses could be categorized into. Then we did some analysis for each industry: for this first pass, we deleted any industry that had very few responses.

Which Are the Most Innovative Industries?

Table A.1 Most innovative industries

Rank	Industry	Innovativeness (Max = 30)	Rank	Industry	Innovativeness (Max = 30)
1	Education	23.25	9	Financial services	21.11
2	Automobile	23.00	10	Health care	20.53
3	Electronics	23.00	11	Government	19.33
4	IT	22.88	12	Service	18.58
5	Marketing	22.75	13	Apparel & accessories	16.33
6	Retail	22.64	14	CPG[2]	16.00
7	Food & beverages	22.52	15	Hospitality	14.33
8	Manufacturing	21.35			

Note: This table lists each industry's highest scoring and lowest scoring dimensions. So, for example, employees of the auto industry rated it high on personal creativity, informal networks, market orientation, and collaboration, and low on flexibility and resources.

---

[2] Consumer packaged goods (CPG) is an industry making products that customers consume and replace on a frequent basis. Examples include cosmetics and cleaning products.

Table A.2 Best and worst dimensions of innovation culture by industry

Industry (Alphabetical order)	Best dimensions				Worst dimensions	
	Personal creativity	Informal networks	Market orientation	Collaboration	Flexibility	Resources
Auto	√	√	√	√	√	
Education	√	√			√	√
Electronics	√				√	√
IT	√	√	√		√	
Marketing	√	√	√		√	√

Some observations:
- Only two of the top five industries seem to set aside resources for innovation. That's surprising. It also makes one wonder how much more innovative the other three would be if they did!
- Informal networking seems to be a hallmark of the top five innovative industries. This seems like a validation of the dimension itself, especially considering it is not something most people would expect to influence innovation readiness.

How Do Things Look by Dimension?

Note: This table lists the industries scoring the highest and lowest for each dimension. So, for example, the auto and education industries provide a lot of freedom to employees, while employees of the CPG, hospitality, and apparel industries seem to miss freedom.

Table A.3 Best and worst industry for each dimension of innovation culture

Dimension	Best (Industries scoring highest on this dimension)	Worst (Industries scoring lowest on this dimension)
Freedom	Auto, education	CPG, apparel & accessories, hospitality
Empathy	IT, education, marketing	CPG, apparel & accessories, electronics
Collaboration	Auto, education, manufacturing	CPG, apparel & accessories, retail
Personal creativity	Auto, marketing, education	CPG, health care, hospitality
Informal networks	Marketing, auto, hospitality	CPG, health care, apparel & accessories
Market orientation	Auto, marketing, retail	CPG, food & beverages, apparel & accessories
Innovation focus	Electronics, IT, government	CPG, apparel & accessories, hospitality
Processes	Auto, IT	CPG, apparel & accessories, hospitality
Flexibility	Food & beverages, IT, financial services	Electronics, hospitality
Resources	Auto, IT	CPG, hospitality

About the Authors

Sanjay Puligadda, creator of InnoQ™, is Associate Professor in the Farmer School of Business, Miami University, Ohio. He teaches, researches, and consults on innovation and marketing. Besides publishing academic research in the leading scientific journals of his field, he is an innovation consultant, speaker, playwright, and improv actor. He received his PhD in marketing from the Pennsylvania State University.

Don Waisanen is a Professor in the Marxe School of Public and International Affairs at Baruch College, City University of New York. He researches, teaches, and consults on communication and leadership. He is the author of seven books, including *Leadership Standpoints* (Cambridge University Press) and *Improv for Democracy* (SUNY Press). Don received a PhD in Communication from the University of Southern California.

Index

Concise and Applied Business Books

The Collection listed above is one of 30 business subject collections that Business Expert Press has grown to make BEP a premiere publisher of print and digital books. Our concise and applied books are for...

- Professionals and Practitioners
- Faculty who adopt our books for courses
- Librarians who know that BEP's Digital Libraries are a unique way to offer students ebooks to download, not restricted with any digital rights management
- Executive Training Course Leaders
- Business Seminar Organizers

Business Expert Press books are for anyone who needs to dig deeper on business ideas, goals, and solutions to everyday problems. Whether one print book, one ebook, or buying a digital library of 110 ebooks, we remain the affordable and smart way to be business smart. For more information, please visit www.businessexpertpress.com, or contact sales@businessexpertpress.com.

Made in the USA
Monee, IL
16 October 2022

16008681R00095